A PARENT'S GUIDE TO
HELPING
TEENAGERS
IN CRISIS

Rich Van Pelt and Jim Hancock

"Decades of effectively working with youth and their parents shine through every page of this outstanding book. With compassion and precision; wisdom and love, Rich Van Pelt and Jim Hancock pack this with illustrations, examples and tools that will guide parents when they need it the most. Parents of children with suicidal thoughts, bullying, and drug abuse are given hope, action plans and clear responses that are most likely to be helpful.

The shelves are filled with Christian counseling books. And there are many books that are helpful in dealing with teen issues. However, *A Parent's Guide to Helping Teenagers* provides a psychological foundation combined with a rare clarity in describing the options and responses that are open to parents in crisis.

Parents have no need to wait until their child has an actual crisis to find this book useful in understanding their teen."
—**Foster W. Cline, M.D.**

"Rich Van Pelt and Jim Hancock's book is a must read for any parent. Often, I encounter parents who ask questions that are directly addressed in this book. It is not a matter of if a parent will need this book, but when a parent will need this book. This book is a practical and tremendous tool in dealing with teenagers and their unique problems by developing a hands-on approach to dealing , understanding and planning out a course of action for teens in trouble."
—**Carey Casey, Chief Executive Officer National Center for Fathering**

"This is the book I suggest to every parent who has a teen in crisis or wants to prevent their child from at-risk behavior. Rich Van Pelt and Jim Hancock are not only two of America's finest experts on the subject, but their content is compelling and informative."
—**Jim Burns, Ph.D., President, HomeWord, Author of Confident Parenting**

"While our fast-changing culture hasn't made it any easier for kids, it's also gotten a lot more difficult for parents. Because we think it can only happen to someone else, we find ourselves paralyzed when the crisis hits home. Gleaned from years of experience in dealing positively with crisis, this book deserves a prominent spot on every parent's shelf."
—**Walt Mueller, President, The Center for Parent/Youth Understanding and author of Youth Culture 101**

"Crisis will come in one form or another guaranteed. Either your child or a teenager associated with them will be in crisis during their teenager years. I'm thrilled that Jim and Rich have taken the time to help parent's figure out a way to prepare for crisis, cope with crisis and recover from crisis. This is an excellent resource not just for parents, but for anyone who loves teenagers and desires to help them process the circumstances of life with a Godly perspective."
—**Doug Fields, Saddleback Church**

"Rich Van Pelt and Jim Hancock have produced a book that every parent needs to read, not only when a teenager is in crisis, but long before: as in right now."

Stephen Arterburn, founder and president, New Life Ministries; founder, Women of Faith

A PARENT'S GUIDE TO
HELPING
TEENAGERS
IN CRISIS

Rich Van Pelt and Jim Hancock

ZONDERVAN®

ZONDERVAN.com/
AUTHORTRACKER
follow your favorite authors

youth
specialties

youth
specialties

The Parent's Guide to Helping Teenagers in Crisis
Copyright 2007 by Rich Van Pelt and Jim Hancock

Youth Specialties resources, 300 S. Pierce St., El Cajon, CA 92020 are published by Zondervan, 5300 Patterson Ave. SE, Grand Rapids, MI 49530.

Library of Congress Cataloging-in-Publication Data

Van Pelt, Rich.
  The parent's guide to helping teenagers in crisis / Rich Van Pelt, Jim
Hancock.
      p. cm.
  Includes bibliographical references.
  ISBN-10: 0-310-27724-8 (pbk.)
  ISBN 978-0-310-27724-8 (pbk.)
  1. Parenting—Religious aspects—Christianity. 2. Parent and
teenager—Religious aspects—Christianity. 3. Christian
teenagers—Religious life. I. Hancock, Jim. II. Title.
  BV4529.V36 2008
  248.8'45—dc22

2007039360

Web site addresses listed in this book were current at the time of publication. Please contact Youth Specialties via e-mail (YS@YouthSpecialties.com) to report URLs that are no longer operational and replacement URLs if available.

Cover design by SharpSeven Design
Interior design by Mark Novelli, IMAGO MEDIA

Printed in the United States of America

---

07 08 09 10 11 12 • 20 19 18 17 16 15 14 13 12 11 10 9 8 7 6 5 4 3 2 1

✚ DEDICATION

For our (now adult) children who taught us so much

✚ TABLE OF CONTENTS

1.0

UNDERSTANDING
CRISIS

Rich Van Pelt: *This book is for parents. It's especially for parents who find themselves dealing with teenagers in crisis. Everyone wishes there were no use for such a book, and everyone knows that's wishful thinking. So here we are, parents trying to help each other deal with the chaos and brokenness of life as we know it.*

Jim Hancock: This parent's guide is as smart and practical as we know how to make it. We are both fathers; our children now adults making their way in the world. We're both veteran youth workers with decades of involvement among adolescents and families. Between us, we've lived through most everything in these pages and vouch for what we say here from firsthand knowledge. That said, we're the first to admit there's a lot we don't know. So we've included endnotes from sources we believe are credible.

One little wrinkle: For the most part we're writing with one voice here. But from time to time you'll find a story or reflection that's truer to tell in Rich's voice or Jim's—as we did in the previous two paragraphs.

If you're in the middle of a crisis, jump ahead to chapters that address your specific concerns. If you're preparing for the *possibility* of a crisis—or steeling yourself for the next one—the place to begin is understanding the nature and characteristics of crisis. Get that down, and you're halfway home.

1.1 IS THIS A CRISIS **OR ISN'T IT?**

JH: I was having breakfast at the Potato Shack a couple of weeks ago when my wife called.

"I'm bringing Hannah to see you," Susan said. "She found a notebook in Ben's bedroom this morning, and she's panicked."

"Did you read it?" I asked. The tone of her response told me Susan was convinced this was for real. "I'll see you in a few minutes," I said.

The notebook had everything but a skull and crossbones warning people to stay out. Several pages were removed from the front of the book, which was empty except for a short story followed by hand-drawn images of self harm and a post script on the final page to the effect that if we were reading this, that meant something had happened to Ben. The short story described the ritualistic torture of someone very much like Hannah by someone very much like Ben.

I already knew that Ben was abandoned as an infant and adopted by my friend Joseph and his former wife, who subsequently abandoned Joseph, Ben, and his siblings. Ben has shuttled between his parents' households several times in the last half decade. He doesn't much trust adults in general and women in particular. Hannah and Joseph are newly married.

Hannah told me how she came across the notebook and why she opened it. Ben had repeatedly threatened and taunted Hannah when his father was out of earshot. Having been the victim of domestic violence in an adolescent marriage, this brought out all kinds of ghosts for Hannah. She was afraid to be alone with Ben. Ten days earlier, he left a letter for them indicating he'd attempted to kill himself.

"What should they do?" Susan asked.

"I need to think," I said. "I'd like to read that letter and see his room."

Alone in my car, I called Joseph and asked him to check with the school and find out if Ben was in class. "I'm on my way to your place," I told him. "I read the notebook; I'm going to read the letter. I think you should find out what your mental health coverage is. From what I know so far, if you asked me if I think Ben might be a danger to himself or others, I would have to say yes."

"I'm on my way," Joseph said. "I'll make the call and meet you at my place in 15 minutes."

When therapists talk about crisis as "a period of *disequilibrium* that overpowers a person's *homeostatic* mechanisms," they're just showing off. In plain English, they're saying *crisis throws people off balance for a while*—emotionally, spiritually, mentally, and sometimes physically.

The clinical psychologist and author Gary Collins called crisis "any event or series of circumstances which threatens a person's well-being and interferes with his or her routine of daily living."[1] The subtle truth of that statement is that crisis is a *self-defined* experience. Meaning that a crisis for one kid may be a non-crisis for another.

Think about that for a moment and you'll see it can't be any other way. Like every painful experience, crisis must be endured first-hand. Perhaps you've been asked by a healthcare professional to rate the intensity of your pain on a scale of one to 10, where 10 equals the most pain you ever experienced. Get five mothers talking about childbirth, and one may rate the pain of delivery as a 10 while another rates it a six. Which is it? Well, for the first person delivering a baby compares with the most painful events in her life: It's a 10. The second woman either had a relatively less painful delivery or experienced some other even more intense pain somewhere along the line. Each is describing her own experience of pain, which is all any of us can do because there's no absolute, objective scale for mental, physical, emotional, or spiritual pain.

This is why crisis is difficult to predict (but not difficult to spot). Crisis can be brought on by anything, where *anything* means: "Any event or series of circumstances that threatens a person's well-being." What's more, circumstances that once overwhelmed a person might be more endurable on a later occasion because *she* is in a different space. And the opposite is also true.

This means nobody gets to vote on the validity of another person's crisis. A parent does a great disservice if he dismisses an adolescent's crisis because it wouldn't rise to the same level for him. The heartaches of "puppy love" spring to mind which, think what you will, are *very* real to the puppy. Parents who take their kids' heartbreak too lightly are not only rude—they also may endanger the well-being of the children they love.

Of course there's also no reason to borrow trouble. It's not a parent's responsibility to *anticipate* that something will be a crisis in the future just because a similar experience precipitated crisis in the past. Kids grow and change—parents ought to *let* them (as if we had any choice). It's not a parent's responsibility to expect the worst, but it *is* our responsibility to pay attention and engage sons and daughters who are *by their own definition* in crisis.

If that brings to mind someone whose life is defined by one crisis after another to the point where you doubt he even knows what a true crisis is, that's fair enough. That's partly why we wrote this book: To help parents calculate the stakes in a crisis and act appropriately to help their children survive and thrive when they come out the other side.

And they do mostly come out the other side. Not that it's easy. What parent hasn't lost patience (or courage) and wondered:

Why did I ever believe I could be a good parent? What was I thinking? If you truly engage your kid in crisis, there's a decent chance you'll experience wide-ranging emotions. With any luck they won't all land at once:

- **Compassion.** *I hate seeing my child in pain! What can I do to help?*

- **Fear.** *My child could die! I'm not prepared to handle this.*

- **Resentment.** *Does he think he's the only one who ever faced this? How selfish!*

- **Impatience.** *How long is this going to drag on? Why doesn't she do something to change her situation? It's a simple decision! Choose already!*

- **Trapped.** *What have I gotten myself into? Is this kid gonna be dependent on me forever?*

- **Guilt.** *I'm such a bad parent. This is all my fault.*

- **Anger.** *When is he gonna stop acting like a baby and get this thing solved? He's just taking advantage of me.*

If they're real, there's no sense in denying these feelings—better to be honest with ourselves and confide in other adults who support us and keep us grounded in reality. Some parental emotions say more about our inexperience with crisis than our enduring emotional condition. Hearing ourselves admit difficult emotions can be a reality check about how soon we need to call for help from someone who's in better shape to lend a hand at the moment.

If a less-than-ideal emotional response doesn't necessarily indicate a parent's permanent condition, the same can be said for the child she's trying to help. Crisis does strange things to people, making them think, feel and behave in ways that are out of character with who they most truly are. All of us who've lived through a crisis know this. The rest will learn eventually.

THREE KINDS OF CRISES

Children and other humans experience three kinds of crises:

- *Acute* crises are pointed, painful, and immediate.

- *Chronic* crises are enduring, recurring, and persistent.

- *Adjustment* crises are temporary, transitory, and situational.

The first two terms—*acute* and *chronic*—are borrowed directly from medical diagnosis and treatment.

An *acute* crisis is urgent and severe enough to demand immediate intervention. It presents the possibility of serious emotional or physical danger. Acute crises include suicidal episodes, drug overdoses, serious flights from home, crisis pregnancies, either side of violent physical and sexual assaults, and losing a loved one.

A *chronic* crisis results from persistent, ongoing, accumulated pain. Chronic crises surface in behavior patterns that demand attention and care. Long-term conditions such as physical, emotional, or sexual abuse; parental neglect; and child endangerment sometimes yield behaviors that may in turn become chronic themselves: obsessive or compulsive sexuality, abusing alcohol and other drugs, eating disorders, fighting, high risk-taking, and cutting are chronic crises with dangerous consequences.

Some chronic crises appear to have biochemical roots—Attention Deficit Hyperactivity Disorder (ADHD) and clinical depression, for example. These are medical diagnoses, not parental hunches. But parents are positioned to see the emotional and behavioral cues that call for professional help.

Finally, some crises are described as *adjustment* crises because they express a child's difficulty adjusting to the demands of growing up or adapting to rapid change. Adjustment crises are often expressed by habitual lying, trust violations, communication breakdowns, defiance of reasonable standards and values, and impulsive behavior. Adjustment crises tend to be non-lethal, but they can stress relationships to the breaking point and may precipitate unhealthy alliances with other kids who are acting out (and sometimes an impulsive act can cost a life or limb).

HOW CRISIS AFFECTS PEOPLE

Countless personal, relational, and environmental factors influence how any individual experiences crisis, so it's only a tiny exaggeration to claim that no two people experience crisis the same way. That said, some experiences are common to most crisis situations—*this will definitely be on the test:*

- Crisis takes people by surprise

- Crisis overwhelms

- Crisis awakens other unresolved life issues

- Crisis paralyzes

- Crisis distorts thinking, feeling, and acting

- Crisis paints a gloomy picture of the future

Crisis Takes People by Surprise

What could possibly prepare a teenage girl for date rape? How many families have even minimal emergency plans should a disaster destroy their homes? Show us the parent prepared to hear a judge say his child has been arrested for possession and sale of narcotics. We're never quite ready for some things—this is why we have a category of human experience called *crisis*.

> **JH:** I had 20 years' notice that my father would die from congestive heart failure. That did exactly nothing to prepare me for news of his sudden death: "Uncle Willard found your dad dead in his apartment today." How do you prepare for that phone call?

RVP: When my father was diagnosed with lung cancer, the prognosis wasn't good. The cancer progressed very quickly, and he died in just a few months without much of the suffering that often accompanies cancer. I'll never forget the last day of his life. His lungs filled with fluid, and he ultimately died from suffocation. Our family gathered around his bed and prayed that God would spare him further suffering and mercifully take him to his eternal home. After about six grueling hours, Dad breathed his final breath, and it became obvious that our prayers were answered. Even so—even after praying that he would die and experience relief from his suffering—when he finally did, we found ourselves in a state of disbelief. As much as we think we're prepared for crisis, it seems we never really are.

Adolescents are famous for believing bad things only happen to bad people—or at least *other* people. Teenagers forget—or maybe adults forget to tell them—what Jesus said about the good, the bad, and the ordinary. Talking about people who died when a tower fell on them, Jesus demanded: "Do you think they were more guilty than all the others living in Jerusalem?"[2] They weren't. Jesus said his Father causes the "sun to rise on the evil and the good, and sends rain on the righteous and the unrighteous."[3]

Good things happen to bad people; bad things happen to good people. Much of the time the universe does a pretty good impression of randomness. In the middle of all that, people are caught unaware, unprepared, and maybe unwilling to face *life as it is* and not as they would have it. Hence crisis takes even the most self-aware by surprise.

Crisis Overwhelms

When a 15-year-old finds out she's pregnant, there's a good chance clear thinking may elude her for a while. Denial, fear, anger, wonder, regret, confusion, embarrassment, doubt, isolation—it's a lot to sort out.

If a parent loses the last scrap of trust in her son, the next thing she's likely to lose is perspective. Anger, fear, shame, regret, and resentment may conspire to declare a state of martial law in the household.

The onset of a crisis can short-circuit normal mental and emotional capabilities. A driven, motivated, self-starting, Type A personality may find the most ordinary tasks slipping from his hyper-competent grasp.

RVP: *I was shocked when I found myself incapacitated by situational depression over a work crisis. Here I was, flying in excess of a hundred thousand miles a year, yet I was barely able to pack for an overnight trip. Fortunately, the crisis passed and soon after so did the depression. But it was a sobering reminder of my humanness.*

JH: For the record, I don't believe in *writer's block*. Still, the last time Rich and I wrote together, a cluster of family crises made it so hard to concentrate that I ended up burning all my margin and hitting the *send* button at 11:59 PM the day the manuscript was due. I hate working that way, but what can I tell you? I was overwhelmed.

Crisis Awakens Other Unresolved Issues

When a crisis strikes, other issues come grumbling from the back of the emotional cave—grumpy and demanding food. Suddenly half a dozen other voices join the howl of the immediate crisis. It's no wonder so many people in crisis mutter, "This is just more than I can handle."

Consider: A high school junior loses his part-time job three weeks before prom. In addition to being worried about paying for prom, you learn he's also concerned about completing an English essay on time and finding a store that sells the right trucks for a skateboard he bought on the Internet.

After deciding it doesn't really matter whether you know what a skateboard *truck* is, your natural response might be, "Just a second: What do finding a new job, writing an essay, and locating those whatchamacallits for your skateboard have to do with each other?"

If you're not careful (as in full of care), you may be inclined to dismiss his concerns because you've forgotten what life can be like for a high school junior. Project your own values, perceptions, and experiences onto him and you'll fail to respond to what he genuinely needs (which may end up having little to do with the details of his complaint). It's easy to miss that—in the grip of an immediate financial challenge—he's also trying to cope with two other marginally connected issues. So of course he's thrown off. Given the often-delicate balance of adolescence, the question is not, "Why is this such a big deal?" The question is, "What can I do to help you sort this out?"

Crisis Paralyzes

Crisis stops people in their tracks, sometimes leaving them stuck indefinitely. No one this side of Superman can reverse the clock and alter events leading to a crisis. A lot of kids burn precious energy wishing things were different—so much energy they may not have enough left to take steps that lead to the light—think Miss Havisham in Dickens' *Great Expectations*—stuck in a dark room, wishing for a different ending.

When feelings of hopelessness combine with a short-circuiting of normal operating capabilities—especially if you throw addictive substances and behaviors into the mix—it's enough to grind the most proactive person to an emotional halt. Everybody knows an adolescent who seems stuck at age 11—or age *two*—his emotional growth frozen in time. It's remarkable how often that sort of stagnation is traceable to a crisis the teenager is too paralyzed to resolve.

Crisis Distorts Thinking, Feeling, and Acting

Parents often say of a kid in crisis: *He's not himself.*

Chemical dependencies are an excellent case in point. When a young person abuses alcohol or other drugs, he's likely to undergo personality or behavioral changes. The drug of choice comes to occupy a central place in his life. Over time, he'll do anything to repeat the experience the drug provides, including behavior that was once out of the question.

Profound shame can generate the same magnitude of distorted thinking, feeling, and acting. So can fear...and grief.

> **RVP:** *I've struggled with the American way of death, shaking my head at the craziness of dumping thousands of dollars into the ground with the body of a lost loved one. But then my father died, and my rationality went out the window too.*

Sometimes parents must attempt to protect kids from themselves—insisting they delay major decisions following a loss, heartbreak, or tragedy. Healing takes time—but not *just* time. It's a crude analogy, but it might help to think about crisis as a broken bone. Proper healing requires immobilizing the breakpoint long enough for the wound to mend.

For an adolescent in crisis, a rebound romance, the sudden move to another household, walking off the team, or the snap decision to drop out of school or join the military all carry the potential for extending rather than resolving the crisis. This is not to say that fleeing a toxic environment may not be exactly the right choice to avert further crisis. It's only to say that crisis distorts rational, long-term decision making.

Crisis Paints a Gloomy Picture of the Future

People in crisis question whether things will ever get better. They doubt it. Emotional distress overwhelms their judgment. They feel helpless, hopeless, and hapless—*The Three Hs.*

- Helpless—*This is too much; I can't handle it*

- Hopeless—*There's no way out; this pain will never end*

- Hapless—*I'm unlucky and that's that*

In the grip of The Three Hs, it's difficult to embrace the ancient wisdom: *This too shall pass.* The work of identifying options is impeded by the conviction that the present crisis is unresolvable. The hopelessness shows up as an emotionless quality you can see in her face and posture, and hear in the way she sighs and speaks.

So, is what you're facing a crisis or isn't it?

The answer: *If it's a crisis for your kid, then yes, it's a crisis.*

And if your kid doesn't admit it's a crisis? *If your teenager is overwhelmed; if one circumstance awakens other unresolved life issues; if your child is paralyzed; if her thinking, feeling, and acting are distorted; if she has a persistent gloomy picture of the future...then, yes, it's a crisis—whether she's acknowledged it or not.*

Understanding crisis involves learning to spot when our kids are knocked off balance. It means mastering the listening and talking skills that create perspective; followed by hope; followed by concrete, forward motion to help them regain equilibrium. Understanding crisis involves paying attention to our own experiences in ways that enable us to express empathy for our children who are not better or worse or really all that different from us.

All that is just ahead in this book, but first there's this...

1.2 DANGEROUS **OPPORTUNITY**

RVP: *I once heard a youth worker say, "I love crisis!" I remember wondering if maybe he could use some counseling or at the least some comp time because clearly the man had lost perspective.*

JH: But really, who doesn't enjoy a good crisis from time to time? Well...me for one. A while back I was invited to sit on the sound mix platform at a U2 show. The concert was on youth group night at the church where I worked so I planned to have someone cover for me (knowing no kid would begrudge me the chance to be at the show, right?). But I decided not to tell anyone about my good fortune—I figured it would make a better story if I hadn't made a big deal about it beforehand.

A couple of days before the concert, one of our peer leaders got caught in a lie that led to a terrific blowup in the youth group. I defused the immediate crisis and, in a fit of remorse, the boy said he wanted to come clean and make amends to his fellow leaders at the next meeting. "Okay," I said, swallowing hard. "I'll help you do that." I called the friend who invited me to the concert and said, "Thanks but something's come up in my group, and I think I'd better stay home. My loss."

Well *that* was an understatement. Not only did the kid not come clean; he didn't even come to the meeting. I could have been sitting on the mix deck at a U2 show! And what could I say?

Nothing! I couldn't even bring it up. But I do want to thank *you* for listening all these years later. It feels good to finally share this indignity with my peers... Okay, it actually feels whiney and I'm sorry I brought it up. All I'm saying is *I don't love a crisis.*

We're all busy people. Juggling work and family and trying to serve multiple masters and figure out who we're going to disappoint when there's not enough of us to go around. There's just no good time for a crisis. We couldn't possibly fit one in this week or next. Get back to us early next month; we'll see what we can do...

A lot of parents don't have nearly enough personal margin to truly be there for their teenagers' small crises. And if we don't show up—emotionally as well as physically—we can't help. Only a full-blown, all-bets-are-off potboiler of a crisis can break into the packed calendar of way too many parents who would say for the record that nothing is more important than their children's well-being. You can probably take it from there.

Crises don't respect the clock or calendar. For what it's worth, the two of us have concluded the *Good Samaritan* of biblical fame hadn't really scheduled the rescue mission that made him famous. That's part of what made him a *Good* Samaritan. He was on a business trip when he dropped what he was doing to look after a man left for dead. If that's how we're supposed to treat our *neighbors* (and the *neighbor* in the story was a complete stranger), doesn't that sort of raise the bar for how we're supposed to treat our own kids?

WHO'S "QUALIFIED" TO HANDLE CRISIS?

Some of us dread—even avoid—facing our teenagers' crises because we're afraid we don't know enough to be effective helpers. We're just parents, right? It's not like anyone gave us any training; they just handed us a baby on the way out the hospital and wished us luck. Sure, lots of us have college degrees (and there's nothing like a specialized diploma to give the impression we know what we're doing), but that doesn't necessarily translate into feeling anything but ill-equipped to help a child in an actual crisis. Qualified? Who are we kidding?

But then there's this. The great Madeleine L'Engle wrote:

> In a very real sense, not one of us is qualified but it seems that God continually chooses the most unqualified to do His work, to bear His glory. If we are qualified, we tend to think that we have done the job ourselves. If we are forced to accept our evident lack of qualification, then there's no danger that we will confuse God's work with our own or God's glory with our own.[1]

When one of our friends was tasked with helping his town's high school community respond to the unspeakable loss of three students in a car crash, he wondered, "How do you prepare for this? What qualifies a person to enter into this kind of pain with kids and families?" If it's daunting for a well-trained youth worker, then why wouldn't it be daunting for the average parent?

RVP: I don't know anyone who's prepared for everything. For more than a decade, I served as a chaplain with the Division of Youth Services for the Colorado Department of Corrections. My youth group was adolescents locked up for every crime imaginable—and a few I found unimaginable. At one point I was asked to conduct a memorial service for one of those young offenders who died after escaping from the lockup. The day before the service I was saying goodnight to a staff member who was particularly close to the boy: "See you at the service tomorrow," I said.

His immediate response was to blurt, "Oh no you won't!"

His reaction took me by surprise and when I asked what he meant he surprised me even more. He told me he couldn't handle the boy's death. Here was an experienced guy who was extremely competent at his job, but his personal fears and inability to cope crippled his capacity to help in that instance.

Plenty of parents understand this dilemma. Death, sickness, depression, substance abuse, and sexual identity are *no-go zones* for some people—*especially* sexual identity. A lot of parents resist the very notion of helping their young folks work through gender identity issues. It becomes clear in a thousand ways that they're not available for that particular duty. Pity. These parents pass by on the other side, leaving their children battered and broken because they haven't resolved their own sexual identities enough to answer difficult questions. Under these restrictive rules of engagement, how will those parents respond if a young person turns up HIV positive (whether the infection was sexually borne or not)? Can parenting be so easily neutralized by immaturity and fear of vulnerability? It can.

Parenting the young and vulnerable can make parents feel vulnerable too. Parenting through a crisis is a contact sport that takes us places we never thought we'd go to address problems we never thought we'd face.

RVP: I've traveled the globe training youth workers, pastors, therapists, school administrators, counselors, teachers, peer counselors, parents—and anyone else who will listen—in crisis prevention and intervention. I typically begin by asking workshop participants to say the first thing that comes to mind when they hear the word crisis.

In my third decade on the road, I can almost predict the responses: emergency, help, disaster, fear, police, danger, predicament, and terrorism. Everyone agrees that crisis evokes images of physical, spiritual, emotional, and relational harm. Few, if any, immediately associate crisis with the word opportunity.

But they could. I haven't had the chance to teach in China yet, but I've learned that the Simplified Chinese characters for crisis combine characters that signify danger and opportunity.

危机

Have the Chinese seen something the rest of the world needs to learn? Do opportunity and danger come wrapped together in the form of crisis? We think they do.

COMING ALONGSIDE

There is a biblical tradition that God comforts the afflicted (and occasionally afflicts the comfortable). God is known as, "the Father of compassion and the God of all comfort, who comforts us in all our troubles, so that we can comfort those in any trouble with the comfort we ourselves receive from God."[2]

It's a nice picture...*The Father of compassion and the God of all comfort.* The writer Earl Palmer says the word *comfort* might be better translated as *coming alongside*, in which case it would read: "The Father of compassion and the God of all *coming alongside*, who *comes alongside* us in our troubles, so that we can *come alongside* those in any trouble with the *coming alongside* we ourselves receive from God." It's a little clunky to read in English but wow! *The Father of compassion and the God of all coming alongside*...Beautiful.

That's what parents imagine when our children are infants: That we'll be filled with compassion and always there for our children—coming alongside to help, no matter what. That's what we ask God to make a reality for us; that somehow, in a miracle of presence when we come alongside our children in crisis, *God* will show up bringing new hope and life from the ashes.

Decades of coming alongside kids and families slogging through life's most difficult terrain transformed crisis intervention into so much more than a duty or interruption in our schedules (and that goes double for our own children). Certainly crisis is permeated with danger—we've always known that. Over time we came to see that crisis is also infused with opportunities for growth.

We don't say that lightly. *Growth* doesn't mean middle-class American fulfillment to us. It means *wholeness*; gradually becoming everything it means to be fully human. We don't know anyone who gets there without considerable pain and more than a few scars from the struggle to truly grow up.

Like the crisis-loving (or at least crisis-welcoming) youth worker whose stability Van Pelt once questioned, the two of us learned to embrace crisis as a means through which grace operates on this broken planet. Please don't misunderstand. We don't take morbid delight in watching kids suffer. On the contrary, truly coming alongside teenagers requires a willingness to suffer *with* them as they suffer (that's what *compassion* means), bringing with us the comfort we receive. We're just doing for kids what we'd want them to do for us if the situation were reversed. We believe we're only giving as good as we already got from *the God of all coming alongside.*

2.0

WHAT TO DO
FIRST

What do you do when the sky falls? What should be your first response and how can you remain responsive long after you've called in reinforcements to help your child in crisis?

This section is about skills to help you assess the immediate risk and then stay connected in the aftermath of your teenager's crisis experience. You don't have to do these things perfectly—you only have to do the best you can do.

Experience tells us that if you learn what's in this section, the-best-you-can-do will actually be pretty good.

2.1 TRIAGE

Back in the day, *M*A*S*H* broke new ground with a mix of hilarity and human tragedy that drew 100 million viewers to its final network broadcast.

Week after week, Radar O'Reilly's voice cut through whatever hijinks were afoot with the dreaded announcement: "Incoming wounded!" followed closely by the sound of helicopter rotors. Doctors and nurses gave each wounded person an initial examination to determine the appropriate medical intervention. Those with life-threatening wounds went immediately to surgery; others less seriously wounded were delivered to a staging tent to wait their turn; the rest were declared dead or beyond help.

That grim assessment process is known as *triage* (tree-ahj), from a French word that means "to sort." Triage is also the first step in helping teenagers in crisis.

Henri Nouwen who, among other things, taught at the renowned Menninger Clinic, wrote:

> We can do much more for each other than we often are aware of. One day Dr. Karl Menninger, the well-known psychiatrist, asked a class of psychiatric residents what the most important part of the treatment process was. Some said the pyschotherapeutic relationship with the doctor. Some said giving recommendations for future behavior. Others again said the continuing contact with the family after the treatment in the hospital has ended. And there were still different

viewpoints. But Karl Menninger did not accept any of these answers as the right one. His answer was "diagnosis." The first and most important task of any healer is making the right diagnosis. Without an accurate diagnosis, subsequent treatment has little effect. Or, to say it better, diagnosis is the beginning of treatment.[1]

Given the natural curiosity and impulsiveness of most children, nine out of 10 parents agree it's a wonder any of them make it to adolescence. Assuming you're reading this because yours have, you've become acquainted with the *Incoming wounded!* alert that announces—no matter what hilarity you're up to—it's time to scramble out to the landing zone to assess the damage and try to figure out your next step.

We say *try* to figure out your next step because the problem may not be as obvious as recognizing a gunshot wound or a compound fracture. This means you may have to work for it.

RVP: I spend a lot of time traveling, and I've always been intrigued by folks who board the plane, find their seat, and immediately begin talking with the person seated next to them. I'm the kind of traveler who prays the seat next to me will be empty. By the time I get on a plane, I'm usually so exhausted that my goal is to be sleeping before the flight attendant starts the safety talk. The last thing I typically want to do is engage in conversation with someone I'll probably never see again.

So it was unusual that I even noticed a woman seated next to me giving every indication that things were not well with her soul—or any other part of her. I was going against type when I asked, "Are you okay?"

Skipping any pretense of small talk, the woman told me her daughter had just made a serious suicide attempt at school and she was traveling to be with her in the hospital. Part of what made the ordeal so painful was that, until the girl attempted to take her own life, the dear woman was totally unaware of how unbearable life had become for her daughter.

She said it was different when her children were younger and easier to read. There wasn't much the kids got away with and when they demanded to know how she'd caught them, she always answered, "A little birdie told me!"

Once, after a day making Christmas candy and cookies, she sent the kids to get ready for bed while she finished cleaning up the dishes. The kids didn't know a mirror in the kitchen provided an unobstructed view into the dining room where the homemade goodies were stored—and where the family parakeet lived.

She watched with amusement as the seven-year-old tiptoed into the dining room, draped his blanket over the parakeet's cage, and summoned his little sisters to join him for the score. The children filled their pockets until they were satisfied they had enough loot to get through the night. The girls headed for the bedroom while their brother lingered just long enough to take the blanket off the birdcage.

Picture their shock when moments later their mom called them out and demanded they turn over the loot. When the sisters turned to give their brother the stink eye, he threw his hands in the air and shouted, "I swear, I covered the bird!"

Now my seatmate was heading into perhaps the toughest conversation of her life. And this time there was no "little birdie" to let her in on her daughter's secrets.

Someone now long forgotten (by us anyway) estimated that many parents of drug-abusing children have a *hunch* about the abuse two years before acting on it. Two years! And it's not just parents. We've both experienced situations in which we sensed something was wrong with a student or family but for one reason or another we didn't follow through to check it out. The older we get, the more we're learning to trust our gut feelings and intuitions and at least explore to see if there's cause for concern.

Triage is different from a hunch. It's the first step a parent takes when she *knows* there's cause for concern. The faint odor of vomit drifts from her daughter's closet. She spots blood stains on the cuff of one of the long-sleeve shirts her child has taken to wearing all the time. Another parent calls to talk about his son's best friend who has been seen mutilating small animals.

These are not *gee-I-wonder-if-there's-a-problem* situations. There is a problem. Job number one is finding out how great the risk is so you can determine the best course of action.

CREATE A SAFE PLACE

Your heart rate spikes when your son says his girlfriend is on the way over and they really need to talk to you. You tell yourself that's silly; they're good kids...but you know very well that's no guarantee against bad news. A few minutes later he's showing her in, and you can see she's been crying, so you brace yourself. "So...what's going on?"

She wells up instantly, and he's barely audible when he responds, "She's gonna have a baby."

You try not to flinch. You warned him about this. He told you not to worry. *Calm down,* you think. *Ask a question. You can kill him later.* "Tell me...more," you say quietly.

What you hear next banishes your anger in a heartbeat—or at least shifts it. This pregnancy is the result of incestuous abuse by the girl's stepfather. The situation is completely different—and still just as bad as you feared. You breathe a wordless prayer of thanks that you chose to ask questions first and shoot later.

Helping your child requires creating a safe place by—

- Getting the facts

- Taking time to listen to the whole story

- Building trust (on top of the trust you already share)

- Allowing for the honest expression of feelings

- Assessing the level of immediate risk

- Evaluating how far you can take the crisis before calling for assistance

Get the Facts

You can respond in a vacuum, but it'll probably just suck. *Triage* begins with gathering basic information to make initial decisions about how to proceed. Of course that means asking for the facts. It also means seeking to understand each person's *perceptions* about the facts.

People have difficulty presenting facts with complete objectivity because no one experiences life objectively. That's even more the case when emotions and thought patterns are distorted by crisis. An experience filtered through the perceptions of two individuals can make you wonder if they're even talking about the same event.

JH: My wife and I once agreed to meet in the lobby of a hotel in downtown Denver. I showed up in a timely manner and waited. Then I waited some more. This was back when cell-phone calls cost 25 cents a minute (or any part thereof) and there was no text messaging, period. We weren't yet in the habit of calling each other 10 times a day. But after half an hour, I started to worry and called her cell. "Where are you?" I asked.

"I'm in the lobby," she said. "*Waiting*. Where are you?"

"I'm in the lobby," I said, looking around. "Right beside the statue of the horse."

"I'm in the lobby and there's no horse," she said. "What hotel are you in?"

"The Adam's Mark," I replied, chilly now. I knew which hotel we agreed to meet at. "What hotel are *you* in?"

"I'm standing right next to the check-in desk at the Adam's Mark, and you're not here," she said. This is when it occurred to me that, although I could think of no reason for such a thing, I'd better check to see if there were two lobbies at the Adam's Mark. There *were*, an employee told me, as if anyone should know this, two lobbies on opposite sides of the street. We were both *waiting* as promised with no hope of actually meeting.

Sometimes you just have to keep asking until you hit on the right question and you begin to understand.

> *RVP: Sometimes I tell a student, "I think I understand what you believe happened. If I were to ask your teacher about this, what do you think she would say?" More than once I've heard the student offer an entirely different account of the event as he imagined it might look through the eyes of his teacher. But that still remains at the level of speculation. The student may have a distorted notion of what his teacher thinks and feels. He might, for example, base his assessment on a tone of voice he perceived from the teacher. A tone of voice—that's a bit like mind reading, isn't it?*

This is why it's important to get more than one perspective if you can. That's not always possible, but it's worth a try. When a kid in crisis says, "My teacher hates me; there's nothing I can do to change that," be generous, but don't take his word for it. He's in crisis. His thinking and emotions may be distorted. If he resists your attempts to gather as many facts and perspectives as possible, it may indicate a deeper problem—or at least a different problem—than the one you think you're working on. Get the facts. Facts are the raw material for solving the problem.

Take Time to Listen to the Whole Story

Jumping to conclusions is not only unfair; it can also be dangerous if it drives an already-at-risk youngster into the night without getting help. There is no shortcut to listening to the story—the whole story. And listening takes time.

Sometimes listening also takes a bit of coaxing. Here's a list of prompts to get the ball rolling. (Note: These questions are not sequential, and not all of them fit every setting.)

- Tell me what you need to talk about.

- Tell me where the story begins.

- Who else is involved in this story? How are they involved?

- Who else knows about this?

- How have you managed to cope until now?

- Who is supporting you through this?

- If you were your friends, would you be worried about you?

- Say more about that.

- Have you considered hurting yourself or someone else?

- Are you taking your meds on schedule?

- How helpful is that? (Put it on a scale of 1 to 10.)

- Tell me more about that.

- Are you self-medicating?

- Talk more about that.

A kid may test the waters to see if you're really interested and able to help or just compiling a case against her. This test could come in the form of a *presenting problem* that has little to do with the core issue—though in fairness, she may not have accurately identified the core issue yet. So without dismissing what *seems* to be the matter, move the conversation deeper—one layer at a time—until your child feels safe enough (or aware enough) to tell *the story behind the story*. (More on this soon.)

Once you believe you understand the presenting problem ask, "And how's everything else going?" Pay close attention; the answer may confirm that the presenting problem is all there is. But it's remarkable how often that question leads to the real issue hiding behind the presenting problem.

In situations where the presenting problem is something like *I'm depressed, I feel alone, I'm confused, I'm tired all the time, I can't concentrate, I just feel sad, I'm always losing my temper, I can't sleep, I just don't care anymore, I can't eat, or I can't stop eating,* ask, "When was the last time this *wasn't* a problem? Tell me about that."

Remember, this is *triage*, not surgery. You're not solving the problem right now; you're taking time to listen to the whole story so you understand what the problem is (or maybe what the problems *are*).

Build Trust

Perhaps you know the old story about the soldier who, before returning home from combat, called his family to ask if he could bring a friend for an extended visit. They responded enthusiastically until he provided more detail: "My friend was hit by a grenade that blew off one of his arms."

Although hesitant, the soldier's folks still encouraged him to bring his buddy home. "You should also know that he lost a leg in the attack," the young man added.

There was a long pause, but they still encouraged him to bring his friend. "I think you should also know he's pretty disfigured; shrapnel tore up the left side of his face."

"Well, you know," his father said thoughtfully, "maybe it would be better if you came alone for a while. Once things stabilize, we can talk about your friend coming to visit." They heard a *click* on the other end of the line.

A few weeks later the soldier's family received notification that their son's body had been found, the victim of an apparent suicide. Confused and wanting to be certain it was really him, the soldier's father asked how positive identification was determined. The officer said the young man had no ID, so they used dental records. "Why," replied the father, "couldn't you have just used a photo from his file?"

The officer's response was devastating. "Sir, your son sustained severe injuries in combat...I assumed you knew. He lost his right arm and his left leg. I'm afraid his face was so disfigured by the blast that a photo would have been of little help."

You can see where the story leads. We all want to know if there are limits to our family's love. Teenagers sometimes fear that if we *really* knew the truth about them, we'd want nothing to do with them—which is sometimes how it turns out.

What a contrast that is to the God people like us claim to know something about. "Be merciful," Jesus told his followers, "just as your Father is merciful."[2] This is the Father about whom the poet David wrote, "The Lord is close to the brokenhearted and saves those who are crushed in spirit."[3]

That's how high the bar is set for parents as we draw out the stories of brokenhearted and crushed children. God help us provide a safe place where they can find hope and healing.

JH: Families that depend on keeping secrets are ticking bombs. If that describes your family, take inventory of your secrets and start opening those doors to your children. I've written about this in a book called *Raising Adults:*

In order for a room to feel safe, somebody has to go first.

Going first means abandoning the party line and telling my real story. It means coming clean. Making a room safe is as simple and as complicated as that.

Parents ask, "How much should I tell my child?" In my opinion, before it's over you should tell your child everything.

Ooh, I don't know. Everything? What if he thinks that means it's okay for him to do some of the things I wish I could take back?

Yes. Everything. If you did something regrettable or even bad, your kids won't think that makes it okay for them. It will help them understand better how you came to be so screwed up—it may serve as a cautionary tale. And it may make it safer to admit their own shortcomings. So, yes, tell them everything in age-appropriate doses. I have. Bit by bit, as Kate got older, I told her more and more. By the time she finished college, she knew the stories behind most of my stories.

What she doesn't know, because she doesn't need to know, is every detail of those stories because many of the details are useless to her. But as my 12-Step friends say, admitting the exact nature of my wrong is quite useful—to her and to me. *The exact nature of my wrong* is far more instructive than the details could ever be. Kate might tell you I crossed the line here or there with too much detail, and she would be right. Learning how to tell the truth of my story without confusing *truth* with *detail* is taking some time.[4]

If you want your children to trust you when they face a crisis, trust them with your stories.

Allow for the Honest Expression of Feelings

Younger teenagers, especially boys, have difficulty articulating their feelings. It's not unusual to hear wide-ranging, even conflicting emotions—especially in matters of family—encompassing intense love and hate for the same person. These emotions are clearly at odds, and they're just as clearly *real*. They must be faced, expressed, and unpacked for healing to take place.

A listening parent can complicate things by agreeing too quickly or by prematurely assessing an emotional expression. Imagine hearing your son's girlfriend talk about being victimized by her stepfather. She's trying to express herself when suddenly it all seems too much for her, and she growls, "I hate him; I wish he were dead."

You might be inclined to respond, "And I'd like to help you bury him." That response might be an honest reaction but it probably wouldn't be very helpful in the moment. Your goal in *triage* is drawing out honest emotional expressions from the adolescent. Don't hijack that. With the next breath she may be preparing to say, "But I love him too much to hurt him, and I'm afraid he's going to get in trouble."

Conflicted emotions are difficult to feel—let alone admit and express—and they can't be explored until they're identified. Invite the open expression of complicated emotions—then stay out of the way while the complications emerge, uncolored by your assessment. (Remember: This kind of listening takes time.) The emotional and spiritual release that may accompany an honest verbalization of such deeply felt conflict could be therapeutic in and of itself.

Use open-ended, guiding questions to keep the process going. To help a teenager in crisis go deeper, say things such as—

- And what did you feel then?

- Talk about your other feelings.

- What did you think she was trying to do?

- What did that make you want to do?

- What else might help me understand?

Of course, finding the words to express feelings isn't easy for people who don't have a reliable emotional map. You can use the emotional map in appendix 6.3 to help kids zero in on complicated emotional territory. The clearer the emotional description, the nearer you are to finding an appropriate next step.

Assess the Level of Immediate Risk

Creating a safe place includes—

1. Not blowing things out of proportion by assigning too high a risk factor for the circumstances

2. Demonstrating that you take your child seriously by testing the level of risk

Expressing care sometimes takes surprising, even counterintuitive forms.

You've just heard your daughter's confession: She was caught cheating on a midterm in the last semester of her senior year and she is mortified. She's been accepted at a major university, but failure to pass this subject would mean not walking with her class at graduation. She also faces the loss of a scholarship from her grandmother's sorority. Knowing you're disappointed—how could you not be?—she murmurs she might be better off dead...at least then she wouldn't dishonor the family. You've never seen her so despondent; never heard her talk this way. What if she actually is suicidal? Swallowing hard, you say, "You know, if I were in your situation and felt as bad as you feel right now, I think I might consider killing myself. Is that something you've toyed with?"

Strange as it seems, by initiating the question, you communicate two important things:

1. You acknowledge how bad she feels

2. You show you're not afraid to explore the emotional depths with her

When you do this, one of two things will happen: She'll either say *yes, she has toyed with thoughts of suicide* or she'll say *no, she feels bad but not self-destructive.*

The next section is about what to do if you're not absolutely convinced that your child has ruled out all suicidal intentions.

If her response convinces you she's not suicidal (and there's a fair chance she'll be shocked that you'd even go there), then you've still communicated that you take her pain seriously and you're not afraid to enter that pain with her and look for healing. In that case—

- Seize the moment as an opportunity for prevention

- Set up a conversation to see how she's feeling the next day—it never hurts to have a warm conversation to look forward to

- Assure her of your willingness to help her work through the mess she's in—you can't rescue her from the consequences of her behavior, but you can certainly walk with her through the process of making amends

- You've come this far, so just say it: "Will you promise me that if things ever get so bad that you want to die, you'll come to me?" Now, if nothing else, she knows at least one person who doesn't want her to die. Often that's all it takes.

Evaluate How Far You Can Take the Crisis Before Calling in Reinforcements

Right now you may be saying, "Whoa! I didn't sign on for this when I agreed to have a baby." That's fine. A crisis can be a reality check for you—a reminder that if there's a God, it certainly isn't you.

Nobody knows your child the way you do, but that doesn't mean you know everything about everything. Nor do you have to. Parents have to stay involved because God gave us this responsibility and put us in the right place at the right time with the promise to make us the right people for the job, at least this once. Whoever said, "God doesn't use us because we're qualified; God qualifies us when he uses us," had a finger on the pulse of reality. Caring enough to *be there* and *stay there* sometimes means more to an adolescent's survival than clinical expertise.

That said, part of the *triage* process involves knowing when to call for help from someone more qualified to extend care. Once basic equilibrium is restored and the child is no longer in danger of tipping over, effective parents always ask, *Who is the right person to move this intervention forward? Can I take my child where he needs to go? Do I have the skills necessary to help in the long term, or do I need to call for reinforcements?* Section 3.1 is about getting help when you need it.

Not to flog this to death but when someone with better skills or experience is available, you need to entertain bringing that person into the conversation. Helping your child get what she needs is more important than saving face or being the one who delivers the goods. If you doubt that, then you have a different problem to deal with.

2.2 SLAP: **WHAT TO DO WHEN YOU FEAR SUICIDE**

Here's a triage tool to help you assess the risk of suicide. Section 4.19 goes deeper into responding to suicidal intentions, gestures, and acts. For now, it's important to think about what to do first when you fear suicide.

> *RVP: I asked a gathering of students, "How many of you at one time or another have contemplated suicide? It may only have been a fleeting thought, or it could have been something you considered for a period of days or even weeks." Close to half of them raised their hands. That represents a lot of sadness, frustration, loneliness, and depression. But their presence in the room underscores the fact that the vast majority of people who consider suicide find a way to regain their balance and choose life.*

The number of teenagers who actually kill themselves in no way approaches the number who contemplate the act. The incidence of adolescent suicide fell throughout the 1990s—from about 11 per 100,000 in 1990 to about seven per 100,000 in 2003. In 2004, that number rose for the first time in many years, ending the lives of 1,985 Americans under the age of 20; about 250 more suicides than 2003. Those are the latest figures available at this writing, and it's unclear whether that increase is a grim blip or the front end of a tragic upswing. What is clear is the insufferable loss of any child who dies at her own hand.

We never dismiss or trivialize suicidal thoughts and intentions. When we see or hear something that makes us feel concern, we employ a simple, time-tested tool for assessing risk. If your teenager expresses suicidal thoughts or intentions, you can use this tool to determine whether you need to take immediate steps to protect his life. It's the simple acrostic SLAP.

SLAP

S—Specific Details

- Is there a specific plan?

- How well has he thought through the plan?

- Has he determined a time? A place? A method?

- On a scale of 1 to 10 (1 = *I would never kill myself* and 10 = *As soon as I have an opportunity, I'll end my life*) where would he place himself? (You may not believe that a kid who's thinking about killing himself would tell you the truth, but there's a high likelihood he will if he's starting to believe he has nothing to lose.)

L—Lethality of Method

- Does the method indicate a clear desire to die? (For example, guns and jumping are more often lethal than taking pills.)

A—Availability of Method

- If the method includes a gun, poisons, or other lethal measures, are those means accessible in your household or are they otherwise readily available?

P—Proximity to Helping Resources

- Does the plan involve a location where he might be difficult to reach?

- Does the plan indicate that he does not want to be interrupted?

- Can he name someone who would want to stop him if he tried to kill himself? A person who has difficulty naming such a person is at high risk. He may be wrong in his assessment—but if he believes it's true, he may *act* as if it were true. If he identifies one or more people who he believes would stop him if they could, that tells you whom to involve in a suicide watch.

It's perfectly acceptable to express your fear and sorrow, but don't freak out. SLAP is played out by asking difficult questions in a manner that is both direct and relationally warm. Your child's responses will help you assess the apparent seriousness of intent, which in turn will help you narrow your options and take appropriate action.

If his responses convince you he's not suicidal, you'll have communicated that you take his pain seriously and you're not afraid to enter that pain with him and look for healing. Let that conversation be the launching pad for a renewed level of communication between you.

If you're not satisfied with his responses, seek medical intervention immediately. Put him in the car or call a cab and drive him to a doctor's office or emergency room. If you feel you need to restrain him, then get one or more adults to accompany you and make him sit between them. If necessary, call 911 for an ambulance or law enforcement agent. They'll ask you if your child is a danger to himself or to others. Tell them *yes* in no uncertain terms. Even if your child hasn't harmed himself, medical personnel will know what to do. (This is step one. Read section 4.19 for more on suicide.)

2.3 CONNECTING

Robert Veninga knew something about people in crisis—he was after all a hospital administrator. But it wasn't until Veninga faced a
crisis of his own that he launched a longterm study to track the differences between people whose lives are ruined by crisis and those
who not only survive but go on to thrive in the aftermath of trauma.
In *A Gift of Hope: How We Survive Our Tragedies*, Veninga identifies characteristics shared by survivors, including this remarkable
conclusion: "Almost without exception, those who survive a tragedy
give credit to one person who stood by them, supported them and
gave them a sense of hope."[1]

Think about that... *One person...*

WHO WE ARE IS MORE IMPORTANT
THAN WHAT WE KNOW

*RVP: My friend Todd was ordered to see a court-appointed psy-
chologist. He was an innocent party in his parents' bitter divorce,
and the court was poised to decide who would be the custodial
parent—hence the psychological evaluation. Todd was incredibly
apprehensive. He asked his youth group to pray about his fear
of counseling and stereotypical shrinks. After his initial session,
I asked how things went.*

"A disaster," Todd said. His worst nightmare had come true, beginning with the doctor's opening question: So, Todd, tell me how you're really feeling? "I wanted to tell the guy, 'You give me the creeps and I want out of here as soon as possible!'" Todd said. He refused to go back for a follow-up session.

The doctor was a licensed clinical psychologist. No question about his professional preparation; no reason to believe he didn't know his stuff—it just wasn't the right stuff this time. He couldn't make the connection necessary to give Todd the help he needed.

If that can happen to a professional, then it can happen to a parent. Helping children in crisis requires making the right connection.

Psychotherapists call the working connection between themselves and a client the *therapeutic alliance*. Michael Craig Miller of the *Harvard Mental Health Letter* writes:

> The therapeutic alliance, also called the working alliance, is essential for successful psychotherapy. Of course, common sense dictates that any consulting relationship should involve a strong partnership that enables two people to do serious work. But there is more to it than that. Many professionals believe that in psychotherapy, the quality of the alliance is more important than any other aspect of the treatment.[2, 3]

A parent who lacks a personal connection with his child may not be much help in a crisis. On the flip side, having a genuine connection goes a long way toward overcoming deficits in formal training. So on any given day, *who we are* as parents may be more important than *what we know* about resolving a crisis. For better or worse.

In some ways perhaps this idea fits the chapter on *prevention* (chapter 5.0) because a lot of what we have to say about making connections is difficult to suddenly acquire on the day a crisis erupts: IN

EVENT OF CRISIS, BREAK GLASS. If your child enters a crisis while believing you hold him in contempt, that's going to make it difficult to establish a connection.

That said, even if things are good between you and your child, every crisis requires a fresh connection.

THE ANATOMY OF A HELPING PARENT

Young people in crisis rarely approach a parent they only *hope* will care about their problem. They're drawn to the parent or other adult who has already *demonstrated* approachability and willingness to help no matter what. Here's what that kind of parent looks like...

Humor

The staging area was prepared for the graveside service of a young marine killed in a combat-training exercise. An open-sided tent covered the area with a dozen or so folding chairs for the immediate family. The family arrived and Grandma (an unfortunately large woman) was seated front and center.

Toward the end of the service, the chaplain signaled the honor guard to begin the customary 21-gun salute. Grandma was so startled by the sound of the first volley of gunshots that she literally lifted off her seat. The folding chair, it should be noted, was not engineered for this particular combination of mass and velocity, so when Grandma came crashing back to earth, it collapsed, pitching her onto the ground. Horrified, her six-year-old grandson screamed, "My God, they've shot Grandma!"

There wasn't a dry eye in the place, and for the first time in days, they weren't tears of sorrow. Even Grandma laughed uncontrollably!

There's obviously nothing funny about the loss of a loved one, nothing comical about terminal disease, sexual abuse, or crisis pregnancy. Laughing at people or the source of their pain is and will remain in bad taste. But sometimes in the middle of life's most difficult moments, funny things happen—and there's something very therapeutic about a good, hearty laugh at the right time. In fact, when we really laugh (the kind of laughter that results in watery eyes and runny noses) our brains release endorphins that attach to the same receptors as morphine. Holy laughter is a painkiller. As the ancient proverb says, "A cheerful heart is good medicine, but a crushed spirit dries up the bones."[4]

JH: Five days after the massacre at Columbine High School, the local youth workers asked Rich to host a gathering just for them. The meeting was closed (no media, no out-of-towners) because the locals were exhausted from nonstop crisis intervention and pressure from outsiders. Littleton was crawling with reporters and presumably well-meaning outsiders were coming to *do ministry* on the population—whether they wanted it or not.

My job that night was to help create a safe place for youth workers to share stories about how God was showing up in the middle of fear and pain. Rich's job was delivering the content in this section. When he started with *humor* as a characteristic of people-helpers, there was the briefest catch, the slightest pause, before it seemed to me like a wave of grace washed gently over the gathering. It felt like the whole room relaxed a little—hunched shoulders loosened a bit, and people took their first unrestricted breath in days.

Rich didn't try to be funny; he only opened the door to the possibility that these dear people might smile again soon. And we laughed together; not hilariously maybe, but naturally and generously, as people alive to the mercy of God.

Empathy

A sign on a camp nurse's office wall reads: "Empathy is feeling your pain in my heart." Not bad. Young folks in crisis are drawn to people they believe understand or are willing to work at understanding what they're going through. It wouldn't hurt parents to intentionally revisit our own experiences in adolescence (well, maybe it would hurt a little, but that's the point). Remembering helps us identify with our kids when they struggle.

That said, there's a vast difference between empathy and the arrogant declaration, "I know *exactly* what you're feeling. When I was your age..." The empathetic parent shuts her mouth and takes time to listen while a young person tells his story. Empathy is the very heart of coming alongside.

In *Living Through Personal Crisis*, Ann Kaiser Stearns observes that the empathetic person—

- Does not shock easily, but accepts human feelings as human feelings

- Is not embarrassed by tears

- Does not often give unwanted advice

- Is warm and appropriately affectionate

- Reminds you of your strengths when you forget you have these strengths within yourself

- Recognizes that growth is a process

- Trusts that you're able to come through your difficult time

- Treats you like an adult, capable of making good decisions

- Acknowledges that he is human, too, and shares this humanness

- May sometimes become impatient or angry, but never attacks your character when telling you so

- Is not afraid to question you directly about your feelings of loss

- Respects your courage and sense of determination

- Understands that grief is not a disease

- Has been through troubled times and can tell you this without making everything seem to be about her

- May not be comfortable with a feeling you're expressing, such as hatred or a particular sexual yearning, but tries to understand what the feeling means to you

- Tells you honestly when he is unable to be with you because of problems or needs of his own

- Remains faithful to commitments and promises[5]

Availability

RVP: My sister Ruthann was in labor in Pittsburgh, and I was waiting in Denver for the phone to ring with news of her delivery. I imagined over and over what my brother-in-law would say when he called: "Hey Rich, it's Dan! You're an uncle!"

Dan's call was nowhere near that much fun. "Ruthie's okay," he said, "but the baby died in delivery."

Everyone was in shock. My first inclination was to call the travel agency and get on the next flight to Pittsburgh. Looking back, I wish I'd gone with my gut. Years later my sister would confess that as much as she appreciated my calls, cards, and flowers, she really wanted her big brother with her through that incredibly difficult time. It's one thing to say we care—but our presence shouts it so loud, it can hardly be missed.

When a crisis breaks, pick up your child from school and give her your undivided attention. You can worry later about what you're not getting done or the money you're not making. For most kids nothing says you care like taking time away from your work.

Emotional Focus

Physical presence demonstrates care, but we must be *emotionally* present as well—because we all know it's possible to be physically present but lack emotional focus.

After her father attended a workshop on listening skills, a high school girl reported arriving home one day to find her dad in the living room reading the newspaper and watching television. As she passed behind his mega-lounger, he murmured, "So how was your day, honey?" Not that she didn't appreciate the gesture but she said, "If my dad really wanted to know how my day was, why didn't he shut off the TV, put down the paper, look me in the eye, and *then* ask the question?"

Okay so maybe she *didn't* appreciate the gesture. She went on to speculate that maybe he wasn't capable of doing two things at one time—watching TV and reading the newspaper—let alone really listening to her. She had very little (meaning *no*) interest in being subjected to a workshop assignment designed to make her father feel better about his parenting skills—not unless he got personally engaged. She wanted to know by his posture that he was genuinely interested in her day.

Our friend Mike Yaconelli was fond of saying the spiritual gift of teenagers is *crap detection*. As much as they long for authentic connections, kids resent (and reject) manipulative techniques. You can't get away with feigning interest just so you can check it off the list—not for long.

Approachability

Accessibility is not the same as *approachability*. We know parents who pride themselves on being accessible to their children. They spend lots of time around their kids at sporting events, on vacation and the like without learning much about their deep hurts, fears, and tough times. These folks are physically accessible but emotionally unapproachable.

Parents who are approachable—

- Value the importance of each child and communicate that value through words and actions

- Never willingly embarrass a child in front of others

- Avoid telling or even tolerating gender jokes or teasing about physical characteristics

- Never question a child's sexual identity and always chide those who do

- Never belittle children who lack physical prowess

- Can be trusted to keep a confidence

If any of this sounds uncomfortably familiar, put a stop to your misbehavior, make amends, ask for do-overs, and work at becoming the sort of person your child will approach in a crisis.

Resourcefulness

People in crisis feel like passengers on a runaway train careening through a moonless night. They hold on for dear life as the train picks up speed in the terrifying dark. Every bump and curve reminds them how utterly and totally out of control they feel—up to a point. Past that point the passengers expect to die; they ride grimly on, wishing it could be over sooner rather than later.

In a rousing action/adventure movie, this is where the hero shows up—godlike from the outside—bringing new hope. "Hold on," he says, "I'll help you get off this thing alive!" This is what kids hope their parents will do; and if we're not in the grip of the crisis too, we can bring clearer perspective and greater capacity to identify solutions than those caught in the middle of it.

> **RVP:** *A youth worker I was helping through a rough spot said, "Having done this for as long as you have, there's probably nothing you haven't dealt with." I chuckled and responded that just when I think I've heard everything, something new surfaces. But my friend wasn't far off. My experience helping students*

and families in crisis makes me unusually resourceful. I'm not bragging; I'm just saying I haven't become less effective with time (despite the wags who remind me the first word in youth worker is—well, you can read it yourself).

You're the adult! Leverage your life experience and what you've learned from past crises to help your child now. If that means disclosing failures you'd rather your child didn't know about—so what! Let your past be a resource to secure your child's future.

Knowledge

Just because who you *are* may be more important than what you *know*, that doesn't mean what you know is unimportant. You're aware of this or you wouldn't be reading this book.

What else can you do?

- Are you certified in CPR? It's not hard; just ask around.

- Are you reasonably current on adolescent development and issues? Download Jim Hancock's eBook *Raising Adults*[6] for a refresher.

- Do you pay attention to what's happening among adolescents in your community? Section 5.2 includes tips on how you can engage other stakeholders in your child's well-being.

- Youth ministry organizations, such as our friends at Youth Specialties and Homeword, host training events to help youth workers and parents understand their teenagers.

- Colleges, universities, civic organizations, hospitals, and nonprofits sponsor useful— and oftentimes free— workshops on adolescent issues. Get yourself a partner or two and take turns going to those events.

Servant Spirit

RVP: I took a group of students to work at Centre Siloe, an orphanage founded by Tony Campolo in Haiti—the poorest country in the Western Hemisphere and regarded by many as a fourth world nation because it lacks the resources to sustain itself.

Living standards in Haiti are worlds apart from what our American teenagers are accustomed to. The cement walls and floors of the orphanage were caked with what seemed like years of filth. The temperature hovered in the high 80s, and the humidity must have been 90 percent or more. The orphanage staff decided our group could be the most helpful if we spent the week cleaning and disinfecting the facility. Not a pleasant job, but our group asked to be useful, not comfortable.

When the orphanage overhaul was complete, one of the high school guys admitted he was relieved we weren't asked to clean the toilets. The receptacles in question were as crude as your typical national forest latrine, but just having an indoor bathroom was relatively uptown in that part of Haiti. The 40 children living at the orphanage, plus 400 more who attended the day school, gratefully used the facilities early and often. So no one had to stick his head in the door to know what was in there.

When Chris expressed his relief, my immediate reaction was to assure him that I never would've asked the group to do something that nasty. He was quiet for a moment, and then he responded, "But you know, I'll bet if Jesus were here, that's where he would have started." Perhaps for the first time, Chris and some of the rest of us understood what it really means to be a servant. The American teenagers did a wonderful thing that week, but I sometimes wonder if I robbed them of an even greater opportunity.

Perhaps the most convincing way to show your child that you have a serving spirit (and that you're not just his maid or meal ticket) is taking him with you to serve people who can do nothing to repay your kindness. It's not an unreasonable leap for a child to conclude that your willingness to serve the poor, the sick, the old, and the discarded might transfer to a willingness to help him through a tough spot.

ONE IS ENOUGH

In a crisis, relationship really matters—more than just about anything. Crisis interventions and especially the prevention strategies in sections 5.1 and 5.2 are not nearly so tied to expert technique as to the *therapeutic alliance*—the genuine connection that sets a context for surviving and thriving beyond the crisis. Remember what Robert Veninga discovered:

> Almost without exception, those who survive a tragedy give credit to *one person* who stood by them, supported them, and gave them a sense of hope. [*emphasis added*][7]

If you're anything like us, then maybe you don't have it all together. As you review the qualities of effective crisis helpers—humor, empathy, availability, emotional focus, approachability, resourcefulness, training, and a servant spirit—you may feel you possess only a couple of those attributes—and even those not as completely as you wish. To this we respond: There's always room for growth, but don't underestimate what you bring to the table right now. You love your children. You can stand by them, support them, and give them a sense of hope. If they know you're in their corner, then that alone may make the difference.

2.4 DEEP **LISTENING**

It's no surprise that kids need help—they're *kids*! Which is to say they're young and relatively inexperienced and in need of basic attention daily. Every once in a while they require more sophisticated help with complex physical, intellectual, emotional, and spiritual issues. This is why it takes a village to raise a kid.

The capacity of any adult—parent, teacher, pastor, therapist, physician—depends on paying attention. That means watching, taking time to ask questions, and listening until we understand what our kids are really saying.

Given the ratio of ears-to-people in the world, listening is a surprisingly rare gift between folks who claim to care about each other. At this writing there's no reliable data on how much time parents and adolescents spend in meaningful conversation, but the common wisdom is *not much, not nearly enough*. Listening takes time. Good listeners pay a price. And some parents simply can't—or won't—ante up.

RVP: One day while I was an adjunct professor in youth and family ministry at Denver Seminary, I asked a class to talk about the most influential people in their lives and why those people were so important. In the middle of describing her dad, one student stopped talking, gathered her thoughts, looked me straight in the eye, and said, "I'm sorry, Rich, but you're making me really nervous!"

Obviously I was concerned that something about my demeanor made her feel uncomfortable. So I apologized.

"Oh no! It's not your fault!" she said. "It's just that I'm not used to being really listened to."

Most young people seldom enjoy being *really* listened to by a parent who takes the time, energy, and focus required to truly understand. The psychiatrist and best-selling author M. Scott Peck put it so well:

The principal form that the work of love takes is attention. When we love another we give him or her our attention; we attend to that person's growth. When we love ourselves we attend to our own growth. When we attend to someone we are caring for that person. The act of attending requires that we make the effort to set aside our existing preoccupations... and actively shift our consciousness. Attention is an act of will, of work against the inertia of our own minds.[1]

JH: Rich has often been asked to lead youth worker seminars on *How to Speak So Kids Will Listen.* I suspect the more important subject to master is *How to Listen So Kids Will Speak.*

HOW TO DO IT

Here are five key elements in deep listening.

Unpack Your Own Bag

Any time you find yourself thinking, "When I was young..." is a good time for a reality check. What baggage—useful and useless—do you carry from those days? What you keep with you says a lot about who you think you are and what you think you're doing as a parent.

Your access to what's in your bag at any given time affects the style and substance of your parenting—especially your capacity as a listener. Unpack your bag and see how the contents shape your listening skills.

LIFE STORY. Who you are as a result of your cumulative life experiences can enhance or inhibit your capacity to listen. If you grew up in an alcoholic family system and never got help to work through anger and abandonment issues, that's going to affect the way you listen to your children. Ditto if you survived childhood sexual abuse by getting help to recover from that trauma. Your story has a strong effect on how you hear your child's story.

AGE. No use pretending you're younger or older than you are. It's just a distraction that causes parents to pay too much attention to themselves and too little to the children in their care.

LANGUAGE. The degree of shared vocabulary between you and your child makes a difference in how many questions you must ask in order to understand.

GENDER. The socialization of boys and girls in any culture influences the manner in which men and women learn to hear spoken messages and read nonverbal cues. Don't underestimate that influence when you listen.

EDUCATION. If you're trained in early childhood development, then you'll listen differently than if you're trained in engineering. Adjust for that.

PHYSICAL SURROUNDINGS. Even if you tend to be a focused listener, a room that is noisy, hot, cold, or crowded can make it difficult to pay attention. If you're easily distracted, it's especially important to control the listening environment appropriately.

PERSONAL CONDITION. It pays to take into account factors such as fatigue, illness, and unresolved personal issues in order to stay focused on listening.

PERSONAL FEELINGS. Don't be in denial about this: On any given day, positive or negative feelings about the son or daughter you're listening to will affect the quality of your listening.

Listening with Acceptance

RVP: I have a friend who has to be one of the most naturally gifted listeners on the planet. She has never studied human behavior or taken a graduate course in counseling psychology, but few people I know have Lindy's capacity to help others move so quickly into heart-to-heart conversation.

I've been privileged to be on the receiving end of her listening skills. I've also watched her do her listening thing with others in an effort to improve my own skills. But I have to admit, after careful observation I've concluded that her ability is more a function of who she is than of what she does. Lindy loves and cares for people. She accepts them as they are. Because what she does as a listener flows so naturally out of who she is as a person, people feel accepted and safe enough to share with Lindy who they truly are.

Teenagers need adults who receive them as they truly are. Parents have unleashed a plague of schizoid kids by teaching them to pretend things are better (or worse...or simply different) than they are. Instead of celebrating the marvel of each person's uniqueness—fearfully and wonderfully made in the image of God—we are responsible for creating little "Stepford" children who live in a world of make-believe because they're afraid that if they reveal their true feelings, beliefs, and longings, they'll be rejected.

An ancient proverb says, "The purposes of the human heart are deep waters, but those who have insight draw them out."² Kids who take a pounding from life desperately need parents who listen nonjudgmentally to what they're thinking and feeling.

JH: The judge in me used to care a great deal about why people went wrong. Was it poor judgment? Compulsion? Irresponsibility? Immaturity? Weakness? Were they victims or perpetrators? Over the years I've come to believe that the details of how people got upside down don't make much difference in the outcome of their lives. Did she jump or was she pushed? Does it matter? She's broken—now what?

Broken kids, however they came to be broken, need help evaluating their condition, assigning responsibility where it belongs, and working toward a way of life that minimizes the likelihood of jumping or being pushed again. But it's no good making that evaluation until they've been scraped off the sidewalk *this* time. *Now* is when we can help by suspending judgment and offering acceptance.

Listen to the Whole Person with Your Whole Person

Kids are highly sensitive to signs of disinterest. That's why effective listeners take pains to project an inviting tone of voice, engaging eye contact, and a relaxed but attentive physical posture—all focused on encouraging a young person to disclose rather than conceal the story behind her story. Your task is to listen to your child's whole person with your whole person.

Effective listening begins with the ears. Someone with a keen grasp for the obvious said, "The fact that God gave us two ears and *one* tongue should be our first clue." The same can be said for two eyes to take in the depth of the person before us (with only one tongue to tell them what we hear and see). How about if we agree to a general ratio of two to one (2:1)—where we look and listen at least twice as much as we talk? This assumes we can learn to exist without the constant sound of our own voices.

There's a reason we so easily lose concentration when we're listening to others. Most listeners process information in the range of 300 to 500 words a minute (the rate generally declines with age). But most people *speak* at a rate of 100 to 200 words a minute. This means there's serious excess capacity on the listening side of the transaction. And with excess capacity comes the tendency to daydream, fret, plan, doodle, and—if we're not careful—lose track of what the other person is saying. Just being aware of this phenomenon can help us be more attentive.

Beyond mere awareness of the challenge lies the physics of deep listening:

- Using your eyes as well as your ears, watching for non-verbal cues as well as making eye contact

- Vocalizing unobtrusive encouragement and requests for more information (*mmm, yes, say more about that, ouch, tell me what you think that means...*)

- Leaning toward the person from time to time to communicate intentional presence

This can be hard work. M. Scott Peck said, "Listening well is an exercise of attention and by necessity hard work. It is because they do not realize this or because they are not willing to do the work that most people do not listen well."[3]

People sometimes say one thing with their lips and a very different thing with their eyes. Even in spoken communication, much is hinted at beyond the words through speed, intonation, pitch, breathing, flinching, flushing, eye-rolling, breaking eye contact, foot tapping, rocking, fidgeting, jaw-clenching, weeping, crossing arms and legs, slouching, slumping, rapidly shifting eyes, and staring into space. Forget about those 100 to 200 words a minute: A person in distress may speak much faster—or much slower—or not at all.

A youth worker friend had a girl in his high school group who showed signs of depression and withdrawal, but she was unwilling to admit she was struggling. Believing that one of the best ways to learn about kids is to visit their homes, he wrangled a dinner invitation for him and his wife. After the meal he asked the girl for a tour of the house. She took them everywhere except her bedroom. That seemed odd so he asked if she would mind showing them her room. She appeared uncomfortable as she took them to a door that required a key. Inside they found a space decorated and furnished for an infant. He said, "Oh you must have misunderstood—we wanted to see *your* room."

"This is my room," she said.

Our friend's honest concern released the girl to tell her story: Months earlier when she'd told her parents she was pregnant, they demanded she have an abortion. She was whisked off that same night to a nearby city where the procedure was performed the next day. Both parents warned her it would smear the family name if she told anyone what happened. Two days later she returned to school with a note asking that her absence be excused due to a cold.

But the girl's bedroom reflected her desire to keep the child alive. That youth worker—listening to more than her words—went the extra mile to get at the story behind the story. His eagerness to see beyond the sanitized version of this young girl's life was the beginning of real healing for her.

Listen for the Story behind the Story

Hear the cry of one young person's heart in an excerpt from this anonymous poem.

Please Hear What I'm Not Saying

My surface may be smooth,

But my surface is my mask,

My varying and ever-concealing mask.

Beneath lies the real me,

In confusion and fear,

In loneliness.

I idly chatter with you in the suave tones of surface talk.

I tell you everything that's really nothing,

Of what's crying within me.

So, when I'm going through my routine,

Please don't be fooled by what I'm not saying,

And what I'd like to be able to say,

But what I can't say.

Only you can call me into aliveness,

Each time you're kind and gentle and encouraging.

Each time you try to understand because you really care,

My heart begins to grow wings,

Very small wings, very feeble wings, but wings.

*With your sensitivity and sympathy and
your powers of understanding,*

You can breathe life into me, I want you to know that.

I want you to know how important you are to me,

How you can be a creator of the person that is me if you choose to.

Please choose to.[4]

A skilled listener learns to use questions to clarify what's been said and repetition to confirm that both parties are having the same conversation. As deep listeners we bear the responsibility to remain engaged until what's being *said* and what's being *heard* are the same.

The writer Paul Swets offers a helpful model he calls **ACE** (Attending, Clarifying, and Evaluating):

ATTENDING. We attend to kids by giving focused attention. Attending requires the discipline to listen with everything we are—to take in and process what they say, how they say it, what they choose not to say, and what they find painful to say.

CLARIFYING. Our challenge is to hear what is being said—not more, not less, and not other than what's being said. That calls for clarifying statements and questions from the listener. Regard the classic counseling phrase, "What I hear you saying is..." as an attempt to clarify meaning. Either we heard what was said or not; the only way to be sure is by asking. (That said, it's possible to misuse the phrase. Learning guru Stephen Glenn used to tease: "If I hear you say, 'What I hear you saying...' one more time, what you'll hear *me* saying is 'Good-bye.'" So maybe there's a better phrase; perhaps *Are you saying...?* or *Let me see if I'm hearing you clearly; it seems like you're saying...*)

EVALUATING. This is the action step. How should I respond to what I've heard? Swets says we have several options:

- Ask for more information
- Remain silent
- Express our feelings
- State our opinions[5]

Whichever we choose, the point is to keep listening until we reach understanding.

Listen with God's Help

We've hinted at this without saying it: Both of us (Jim and Rich) believe we need help from God in order to get outside our own skins and pay attention to the needs of others. We'd love to say we're less self-absorbed than that, but there you have it. So in the spirit of trying to *pray without ceasing*, we're in the habit of talking to God while we listen to others: *What do you want me to hear? What do I need to understand? What do you want to do in this conversation?*

Hebrews 13:20-21 reads:

Now may the God of peace, who through the blood of the eternal covenant brought back from the dead our Lord Jesus, that great Shepherd of the sheep, equip you with everything good for doing his will, and may he work in us what is pleasing to him, through Jesus Christ, to whom be glory for ever and ever. Amen.

We believe people who depend on God really can be equipped "with everything good" for doing God's will. The God who calls us to *come alongside* our children in pain with the same *coming alongside* we ourselves have received from God will *equip us and work in us* what is pleasing to God.

We don't believe we're called because we're qualified—we believe God will qualify us to accomplish what we're called to do.

3.0

GETTING HELP
WHEN YOU NEED IT

Repeat after us: *It's not about me; it's not about me; it's not about me...*

The impulse to control a crisis is understandable—but misguided. Being the right person to begin an intervention doesn't necessarily make you the right person to see it through to the end. You'll need to be there at the end, but you may not be in charge—by which we mean you may NOT be in charge. If you could just step in and fix it, it wouldn't be a crisis. Please don't think you can control the crisis recovery path for your adolescent.

Nothing personal—you're not a physician or a counselor; you're a parent. An effective action plan shifts appropriate responsibility and credit to the person in crisis—your teenager. Along the way be prepared to ask for help from people who can assist your teenager in ways you can't.

Say it again: *It's not about me; it's not about me; it's not about me. . .*

3.1 CALLING IN **REINFORCEMENTS**

No one is capable of *knowing all*, *loving all*, and *healing all*. Effective parents figure that out sooner rather than later, and they often do so when they encounter a situation that requires more insight or understanding than they're prepared to deliver—or maybe the same goods, but delivered by someone else. Take a deep breath and repeat one more time: *It's not about me; it's not about me; it's not about me.*

Calling for help is not an admission of weakness. It's a sign of strength—a statement that you're committed to seeing your child get the help she needs regardless of the source.

When you call for help, do your best to be *responsible, timely,* and *realistic.*

BE RESPONSIBLE

Find a person or agency that's better positioned than you to address the identified problem (or identify what that problem truly is). Your child may feel afraid or abandoned when you bring in outside help, so make every effort to assure him you'll continue to be there for him even though you believe someone else is better positioned to help in the present situation. Let him know that calling for help is not subtracting, it's *adding*.

Ask Someone Who Knows

We teach youth workers to develop a crisis network of reputable therapists, specialists, agencies, and programs to which they can direct families. You probably don't need to maintain such a list yourself, but you need to know someone who does. Ask around your community for a youth worker who takes this task seriously. If that youth worker has done her homework, then she'll do at least these two things:

- Ask about your insurance coverage and other financial resources so as not to recommend something that is simply unavailable to you. Some therapists and specialized treatment programs offer a sliding scale where cost of services is determined by salary level, number of children in the home, and extenuating circumstances. This youth worker will know who is positioned to work with uninsured families.

- Try to suggest more than one therapist or program from which you can choose. When that's not possible (and if you live in a small town, it almost never is), expect her to describe her recommendation as the best resource she knows of locally—as distinct from calling that person "the best in the country or I'll eat my hat!" Which is to say, beware of irrational exuberance from someone making a recommendation.

JH: This afternoon I took a call from a friend whose teenage sister is in trouble in a city where neither of us lives. I called a youth worker in that city, laid out the general situation, and asked for recommendations. He was away from his office, but tomorrow morning he'll e-mail descriptions and contact information for four individuals on his referral list, which I'll then pass along with confidence because, even though I don't know any professional people-helpers in that city, someone I trust does. (In fact, this youth worker used that same list to refer a family in his church just last night.) That's the way this is supposed to work.

Assume Nothing

Unless you face a medical emergency and have to accept the first help available, take a little time to evaluate whether a given professional is the right person to help your child. Professional certification (MA, MSW, MD, PhD, etc.) and a current license to practice are promising attributes that actually guarantee only that a person has passed the right tests and complied with licensing requirements. These are not small things, but they don't assure quality. This is part of what we were talking about concerning the *therapeutic alliance* in section 2.3.

It's unusual but perfectly acceptable to ask for a brief telephone conversation before scheduling an intake appointment. Don't expect to get anything specific out of such a conversation. Instead, ask a couple of general questions about the individual's (or program's) approach to teenagers in crisis and about his or her (or their) experience with adolescents in the kind of struggle you believe your child faces. A young person battling a cocaine addiction doesn't belong in a program that specializes in treating alcoholism. A therapist who specializes in geriatric issues is probably not the right choice for helping an adolescent with an eating disorder.

Keep it brief. If the therapist (or whoever) asks questions, answer briefly and honestly. It's fine to ask about faith perspectives, but don't be put off if the answer doesn't sound like what you'd expect from a pastor. Some therapists decline to talk about their faith with clients because the problem at hand is not about the therapist's faith and certainly not about her personal theology. (On the subject of the client's faith, therapists are more likely to ask questions than make statements.) The important thing to learn in your introductory conversation is whether or not a person or program seems likely to intentionally undermine the faith of your child.

This is a gut check. You'll finish that conversation with a degree of confidence somewhere between zero and ten, where zero equals *There's no way I would entrust my child to this moron.* This is not to say that you'll be right about the suitability of the connection, but at least you won't be flying completely blind.

Ask yourself:

- Did this person seem to know what she was talking about?

- Did she seem to care about adolescents?

- Did she engage me with openness or did she try to intimidate or bluff me?

- Would I be comfortable introducing her to my child?

Then take action. Don't wait for an assurance of absolute certainty (there's no such thing). Exercise your best judgment and get on with it.

BE TIMELY

Call in reinforcements—

- As soon as you sense a situation is beyond your capabilities

- As soon as you believe specialized treatment may be warranted

- As soon as you believe your child may be dangerous to himself or to others

Be prepared for the possibility that your child will resist the help of an outsider—perhaps openly, perhaps by lying or other forms of sabotage. That sort of resistance can often be traced to a fundamental fear: *If I need a therapist, I must be crazy!* The image of a client lying on a couch and spilling his guts to a therapist who is bored and slightly crazy himself is enough to send most teenagers over the edge. Adolescents, like most other humans, don't want someone playing with their heads. This is why it's important to know as much as possible about the people you bring into your child's crisis. (Remember: *Addition*, not subtraction.)

If you come to believe there's a negative relationship between your child and a therapist, don't be afraid to consider a different counselor—but don't jump from therapist to therapist either. Insist on giving ample time for the professional to develop a positive connection with your teenager.

BE REALISTIC

RVP: I took a call from a youth ministry colleague looking for an appropriate treatment facility for a young man in her group. I asked a bit about the boy's history and his present situation in order to zero in on a suitable recommendation. A facility in another state seemed to offer exactly what he needed, and it included a wilderness adventure component that was a perfect match with the boy's love of the outdoors. I agreed to talk with the boy's mom and share what I knew about the program. We had a great conversation; and the more I told her about the program, the more excited she became. It seemed like a perfect fit.

But I made a terrible assumption. Because I had visited their church and had a good feel for the socioeconomics of their community, I assumed there would be no problem with insurance. Wrong. The boy's father had been out of work for more than a year, and the family was without medical coverage. Without insurance, the program I recommended costs $1,000 a day out of pocket—far more than they could afford. In my naïve enthusiasm, I set the mom up for a terrible disappointment. Our conversation shifted from considering a world-class treatment facility to brainstorming community-based programs. I sure wish I could start that one all over again.

"Square one" when you know you need to call in reinforcements is evaluating your financial resources. It doesn't matter how many successful programs exist in your community if the cost is more than you can afford. If you're insured, find out the limits of your coverage. Get your ducks in a row so you can make a clear-headed decision.

Many churches offer pastoral counseling services, and some have full-scale counseling programs in place. Services are typically provided free to parishioners or fees are determined based on ability to pay. Other churches and helping agencies may provide financial assistance so individuals and families in need can receive professional counseling. There's a pretty good chance you know someone who knows about these resources—or can find out.

Whatever the case (we wish it weren't necessary to say this), you should gain a clear understanding of the out-of-pocket costs and payment options before treatment begins.

3.2 DEVELOPING AN **ACTION PLAN**

On a really good day, crisis intervention identifies a problem and solves it—permanently. Other days, success is measured by lessening the impact of something that can't be fixed—developing coping strategies for living with a terminal illness comes to mind. Most days parents split the difference between the permanent solve and making the best of a difficult circumstance.

What's common across the board is the need to help adolescents develop a course of action *they can follow*. The emphasis is important because kids must act on their own behalf or we've only postponed the problem for another day. Parents who make the decisions in a crisis don't help their children learn to identify and work through challenges in the future. That's *rescuing* rather than *coming alongside*. There are rare instances when an adolescent must be persuaded or caused to surrender self-determination temporarily because she's dangerously out of control; but those are exceptional circumstances. Effective crisis intervention always seeks to reestablish the equilibrium that ultimately leads to personal responsibility and appropriate behavior.

Parents who work *with* a kid to develop an action plan poke holes in the darkness, letting in enough light so the child in crisis can see a way out. Since most kids don't have much experience in planning, parents should guide the process without hijacking the plan. At the end of the day, youngsters need to develop a course of action that will renew the balance they lost. It's their work to do because they must live with the choices they make.

In *People in Crisis: Understanding and Helping,* Lee Ann Hoff provides a useful model for evaluating the likely success of an action plan. A good plan should be—

- Problem oriented

- Appropriate to the person's functional level and dependency needs

- Consistent with the person's culture and lifestyle

- Inclusive of significant others and social network

- Realistic, time limited, and concrete

- Dynamic and renegotiable

- Inclusive of follow-up[1]

PROBLEM ORIENTED. A good action plan doesn't try to do everything in one fell swoop. Instead, it focuses on and limits itself to the *identified problem.* The immediate goal is designing a plan to restore equilibrium; therefore, the plan is specific and limited to the problem at hand.

APPROPRIATE TO THE TEENAGER'S FUNCTIONAL LEVEL AND DEPENDENCY NEEDS. Kids function on intellectual, emotional, physical, and spiritual levels that may not be equally matched. (For example, a person may be physically mature but emotionally immature, or intellectually sophisticated but spiritually naïve.) If you've forgotten what it's like to be an adolescent, now's the time to remember. A successful crisis plan is marked by awareness of the functional level of the one who'll be doing the work. Expecting the best of kids should never translate into expecting more than they can deliver—that frustrates everyone involved.

CONSISTENT WITH THE TEENAGER'S CULTURE AND LIFE-STYLE. Effective parents are at least generally aware of the youth cultures in which their children live, and sensitive to the challenges and opportunities presented in those cultures. If we become aware that the subculture in which a kid moves is part of the problem, that will make a difference in the action plan—just as it would if we came to believe that culture might contribute solutions to the crisis. A high school sports culture, for example, can contribute negatively or positively to a kid in crisis depending on the character of the culture and the condition of the kid. All of which is to say, an action plan should be specific to the situation at hand.

INCLUSIVE OF SIGNIFICANT OTHERS AND SOCIAL NETWORK. Effective plans account for the need we all have for support and encouragement. This is especially sensitive for the young person who believes no one cares whether he lives or dies. An old letter to Ann Landers illustrates this well.

Dear Ann Landers:

Last week I attended a funeral visitation. It was extremely sad. A 13-year-old girl had committed suicide. "Sally" was five-foot-two, thin, petite, blonde, and wanted desperately to belong. She tried out for cheerleading and didn't make it. In fact, she failed to get into a single club she signed up for. The girl looked so unhappy, my heart ached for her. A few weeks ago Sally won a raffle. It was a certificate from a pizza place that entitled her to invite 14 friends to a pizza dinner. She turned down the prize because she said she didn't have 14 friends. At the funeral home, I sat and watched the school kids come through in droves. I counted well over 100 students in the 45 minutes I was there. Later I learned that more than 100 had signed the guest book.[2]

Whoever said, "Friends are the lifeblood of adolescence," got it right. In tough times who hasn't appreciated the encouraging words and physical presence of people we call friends? A good plan finds ways to rally the troops around a hurting kid in authentic, appropriate ways.

That said, an effective plan also recognizes that an adolescent's social network may be a contributing—even a primary—negative factor in the crisis. A young person struggling with drug dependency will have difficulty kicking a habit while she associates with friends who are users.

REALISTIC, TIME-LIMITED, AND CONCRETE. What good is a plan with no anchor in reality? It can only raise false hopes and expectations. It's important to calculate the possibilities *and* the limitations of the plan so the established goals are attainable in a reasonable time frame.

Agreeing to a time line is an effective means of motivating people to action. An agreement with no dates attached is more *notion* than plan. A time line grants mutual accountability.

Make certain the plan is *concrete*—meaning specific and easily understood. If you agree you will all learn to cooperate, help your child translate the fuzzy *learn to cooperate* into concrete, *measurable skills such as learn to listen respectfully to each other* and *learn to find win-win solutions when we disagree.*

DYNAMIC AND RENEGOTIABLE. Life is never static. As people and situations change, the action plan may need updating or replacing with a new and timelier plan. Let's put a smiley face on it: Sometimes folks "get it" faster than anyone thought possible. If that happens, agree to skip ahead in the plan—as long as everyone is confident it's true progress and not just a bluff.

INCLUSIVE OF FOLLOW-UP. If you help your teenager develop a responsible action plan, it's important to evaluate the process together, to shore up weaknesses and celebrate successes together. Agree on time intervals for follow-up.

WORKING THE PLAN

An unimplemented plan is just a collection of ideas. If the goal of crisis intervention is resolving the immediate crisis or at least lessening its impact, the effectiveness of the plan can be measured by the degree to which it moves everyone toward those ends.

It's frustrating to do the hard work of constructing a plan only to see it sabotaged or abandoned. Here are the most common reasons adolescents fail to follow through.

Lack of Capacity

Crisis overwhelms kids, short-circuiting normal functioning capabilities. A bright, capable young person may have very good intentions but find herself emotionally or psychologically incapacitated. Here's where the excess capacity generated by your age and experience will come in handy. If you're tapped out too, it's time to call in reinforcements.

Fear of the Unknown

An adolescent may continue making the best of a bad thing if he fears that taking action will result in an even greater loss of control. This is true for the abused child who's old enough to know what's going on and articulate enough to tell someone who could help, but keeps quiet because he's terrified about the consequences of speaking up. "Better the Devil We Know" is the name of that sad tune. If you believe your child is paralyzed by fear, you may be the one to encourage him—to put the heart of courage into him—so he can do what needs doing.

No Desire for Change

There is a rather bizarre moment in John's account of Jesus, where Jesus asks a crippled man, "Do you want to get well?"[3] It seems like a ridiculous question except for this: Sometimes people appear to prefer sickness to the possibility (and responsibility) of health. The question is *Why?*

Don't read too much into it, but listen for subtle language cues such as speaking of tragedy in the first person possessive—*my rape, my accident, my cancer.* What does a kid get out of hanging onto a problem or generating a succession of crises? Get to the bottom of that and the problem is half solved.

Ownership

Your action plan is interesting but not necessarily fascinating to your child. A kid who participates in designing his own action plan is more likely to engage and follow through, and less likely to sabotage the plan. The greater his personal investment in the process, the greater the chance he'll work to make it succeed.

Lack of Resources

Implementing an action plan requires time and attention and access to helpful people. Do what you can to create a buffer within which your teenager has what she needs to do the work she must do.

Personal Discomfort

There are situations when an action plan requires that kids move well outside their comfort zones. Ask your child to count the cost beforehand, while the plan is being written; then call on him to do what he promised—and support and celebrate his efforts to follow through.

Here's a flow sheet for identifying and sorting the issues and options that form a workable action plan. (It's reproduced in appendix 6.1 and available as a downloadable PDF at www.ys.com/xxx/actionplan). Use the relevant parts of this sheet as you help your adolescent develop a plan to get him from where he is to where he needs to be.

ACTION PLAN WORKSHEET

I. What is the identified problem (beyond the presenting problem)?

II. What are the possible outcomes (both negative and positive)?

   A. Which is the most desirable outcome?

   B. What general steps are required to move toward that outcome? (Return to more specific steps later.)

III. Who are the active participants, and what is their stake in the outcome?

IV. Who are the passive participants, and what is their stake?

(And what can be expected from each stakeholder?)

V. What are the resources and roadblocks to reaching the goal?

VI. Who else should be involved in the solution?

    A. Extended family?

    B. Professional referral?

        1. Medical doctor?

        2. Psychiatrist, psychologist?

        3. Social worker?

        4. Law enforcement?

        5. Lawyer?

        6. Pastor, youth worker?

        7. School personnel?

        8. Employer?

        9. Friends?

VII. What specific steps must be taken?

    A. In what order?

B. Who should take responsibility for each step?

C. Who should provide support?

VIII. What is the timetable?

IX. What other resources are required?

A. Money?

B. Transportation?

C. Temporary lodging?

D. Food?

E. Other?

X. Who will provide ongoing support and feedback?

3.3 *INTERVENTIONS*

When he was director of the National Institute on Drug Abuse, Alan Leshner described the essence of addiction as "uncontrollable, compulsive drug seeking and use, even in the face of negative health and social consequences."[1]

Uncontrollable...compulsive...even in the face of negative health and social consequences... This echoes the declaration from Pastor Don Finto: "What you can't get enough of, that's your god."[2]

There's an element of idolatry in addiction. Granting the chemical effects of drugs on the brain, you can see that in the withdrawal symptoms—if nowhere else—there is also a strong element of *desire* in the user's drug seeking. Addicts are willing to leave father, mother, home, and friends for the drug. They'll lie, cheat, and steal for it. And they'll surrender their bodies to the drug in a complete act of devotion.

This is easier to see if we set aside chemical reactions for a moment and focus on addictive *behaviors*. Sex addicts and codependents don't have physiological withdrawal symptoms from abstinence, but they certainly experience powerful emotional and spiritual suffering that an alcoholic or meth addict would recognize.

Getting the attention of a person who's so thoroughly given over to a substance or behavioral habit isn't easy.

Most addicts don't really contemplate giving up their drugs until they're confronted with the high likelihood that they'll have to give up everything else—family, job, home, car, friendships, personal dignity...everything—in order to keep using. Faced with that, an addict really has to think about cutting back.

There's a story going around that the average alcoholic in recovery (whatever "average" means) figures he got about 54 wake-up calls before he finally admitted his life was unmanageable and only a power greater than himself could restore him to sanity. We can't tell if that's a real number or if it's just a good story about how hard it is for an addict to figure out the drugs don't work (because they certainly *appear* to work—right up to the moment they stop working) and how worthwhile it is to hang in there (non-codependently, of course) with a user who may be on wake-up call number 53.

INTERVENTIONS

We'll italicize the word *intervention* here because everything you do in response to a crisis is an intervention. What we're talking about here, though, is a well-defined process that's come to be known by the name *intervention*.

Interventions are designed to break through denial in people struggling (or maybe not struggling enough) with chemical dependencies and addictive behaviors. *Denial*, as the old joke goes, *is not a river in Egypt*; denial is an elaborate patchwork of excuses, adaptations, rationalizations, and reasons why everything is working much better than it would appear and the ones who are worried are the ones with the problem. Until a user acknowledges her need, she won't be motivated to seek help. (*User* has two meanings here, because addicts tend to use friends, family, even total strangers, as well as controlled substances.)

An *intervention* is a structured time during which people close to the user present her with factual statements that underscore the severity of her behavior as it affects them.

This is important: The *interventionists* tell the addict how her behavior affects *not* her but them (this can be infuriating to an addict, so be prepared). *Interventions* divert the focus from the ego of the user to the impact of her behavior on people who are important to her.

Interventions should include a minimum of two affected people—and more is better because there's safety in numbers. But not too many. If the user feels like you're piling on, she may respond with stubborn defensiveness (which she may do anyway). Or she may simply shut down, believing you'll wear yourselves out and leave her alone if she just goes limp on you.

Effective *interventions* are story-based and nonjudgmental—a facilitator referees to make sure they stay that way. But successful *interventionists* are in no way shy about speaking into the life of the user with specific and detailed personal accounts of what her behavior has cost each person in the room—that's the whole point. The *interventionists* aren't accusing the user of being selfish; they're demonstrating through true stories how selfishly she's behaving (probably without ever using the word *selfish*).

This is tough going. Sometimes the only thing that keeps an *intervention* from getting out of control is true love and the hope, however faint, that the user could live instead of die. Premature death is the eventual outcome of addiction. (Check out the lost years of potential life in section 4.18.)

The facilitator may be an outside mediator brought in to help or she may be one of the circle of friends. Part of her job is making sure each participant has ample opportunity to give specific, real-life examples of the negative effects of the user's behavior. In the process, users hear—perhaps for the first time—about things they did under the influence, how others truly perceive them, and how their behavior has damaged their friends and family.

The facilitation needn't be heavy-handed or even obvious. We've been part of *interventions* where the conversation was guided so subtly that an observer might have had difficulty picking out the facilitator. The facilitator can encourage participants to describe the consequences they foresee happening should the user continue using:

Boss: "One more time and I *will* fire you."

Friend: "And you'll lose your car."

Father: "Because I won't pick up your payments and insurance."

Friend: "You'll have to sell it."

Father: "At a loss because it won't bring what you paid for it."

Brother: "So she'll still owe money on a car she no longer owns? That sucks."

Whatever happens, the facilitator keeps bringing the subject back around to love, committed concern, firm resolve and hope.

Don't rush an *intervention*, but don't let it go on indefinitely. If it's working, the user will probably be exhausted before the *interventionists* run out of things to talk about. If it's not working, there's no sense in beating it to death. There may come a moment when the facilitator must say, "I think we've done what we can do for now," at which point it's good to ask the user to summarize what she's heard so far. Her response may reopen the dialogue, or it may simply confirm what everyone in the room suspects: It's time to regroup and plan another approach.

If that's the case, make sure everyone understands that you're inserting a comma into an unfinished thought, not putting a period at the end of a sentence. There's nothing wrong with setting up another meeting then and there. If the user is still in the room, it's because she's trying not to burn any more bridges—or maybe because the truth is beginning to dawn on her.

The goal of an *intervention* is to break through denial and motivate the user to receive help. The *interventionists* should have a good idea of what that help will look like when they walk in the room.

This is not a good time for brainstorming. If mental health counseling or detox are part of the plan, then you need to know what's available, what it will cost, what it takes to get the ball rolling, and what to do during the hours (more likely days) before the treatment commences.

In evaluating the help available, you'll need to grapple with these questions:

- Is hospitalization likely required for detoxification or other medical reasons?

- Do you think a medical specialist is required?

- What level of family involvement is required in the process?

- Is inpatient or outpatient care preferred?

- Can treatment begin immediately? If not, how long is the wait?

- What is the duration and location of the treatment?

- What will treatment cost?

- What costs will be covered by insurance?

- What is the success rate of the treatment program(s) you're considering?

- Is a peer-based help program like Alcoholics Anonymous a possibility?

If the plan leans toward peer-based assistance, there's a 12-step meeting starting nearby in about two hours—no matter where you are. (For information on finding an AA meeting, go to http://www. alcoholics-anonymous.org/en_find_meeting.cfm.) In most places you'll find a centralized number in the phone book for Alcoholics Anonymous, Narcotics Anonymous, and other 12-step programs. They'll be more than happy to send you a schedule, direct you to a local Web site, or tell you about their meeting times and places.

Since 12-step meetings are not all created equal, learn in advance when and where to find an appropriate meeting. If you don't know anyone working a 12-step program, ask around and someone will find you. That's not meant to be spooky. It's just that Alcoholics Anonymous, Narcotics Anonymous, Sex Addicts Anonymous, and the rest are in fact *anonymous*. They don't use last names, and they don't identify each other in public except by prior mutual agreement. So if you start asking friends if they know where you might find a 12-step program for your kid, pretty soon one of them will say he might be able to give you a phone number and off you'll go.

If the user is a minor, and she continues to deny the problem (or the *severity* of the problem), then you might be legally obligated to arrange for her treatment—whether she wants it or not. This is a rare and difficult thing and if you don't believe you're taking life-saving action, then go back through the user's history and consider the *intervention* options one more time to see if there's another way.

If you're afraid of losing your child by taking such drastic action, we can only hope to encourage you with the news that, though your child may resist and resent your decision, there is little difference in the rate of success between those who voluntarily submit to treatment and those who fight it tooth and nail. Many teenagers dragged into treatment end up expressing profound gratitude for their parents' tough choices—maybe not soon, but eventually. With a little grace you may save the relationship as well as the child.

4.0

CRISIS
COMPENDIUM

These are 22 crises we keep running into in all kinds of families in all kinds of places. Some of them overlap; a lot of them are not as they first appear.

This section lays out background issues and basic action plans as a starting point for *intervention* and prevention.

4.1 ACCIDENTS

When there's an accident with serious injuries or death, the inescapable question for most kids is Why?

- *Why did this have to happen?*

- *Why was my friend (or whoever) so stupid? Or careless? Or unlucky?*

- *Why would God allow this?*

Then it gets personal . . .

- *Why not me?*

- *Why did I decide not to go with them?*

- *Why did I survive?*

- *Why wasn't I injured?*

This is the beginning of *survivor's guilt*—the chief feature of which is an unhealthy self-consciousness: *It **should** have been me.*

There aren't many satisfying answers to the *Why* questions surrounding serious accidents. Coming to accept that fact of life is a necessary developmental task for adolescents. Help your child learn that lesson, and you'll prepare him for a world of grief later. If that sounds a little grim, the alternative is that he'll have to endure grief without any help from you.

We don't believe God wastes pain. We don't believe parents should either.

ACTION PLAN: ENGAGE THE PAIN

Don't over-explain, but when the time is right—with gentleness and respect and without preaching or exploiting your child's brokenness—engage her in exploring and learning what she can from the tragedy.

- If the accident resulted in death, create a safe environment for storytelling and recollections about the one who was lost. If it's appropriate, encourage your child to invite friends over to decompress together.

- Without hijacking or competing for air, recall stories of accidents and grief in your own life.

- Don't bluff. Thoughtful adolescents are not much comforted by glib assurances that everything happens for a reason—nor should they be. It's tempting to fill uncomfortable silences with platitudes, but kids need honest, thoughtful reflection. When you don't know what to say, let silence do its work. "I don't know why this happened" is better than "I guess his time was up" or "God has a purpose for everything."

- If an accident results in lengthy hospitalization or disability, teach your child basic hospital etiquette. (Rule of Thumb: Unless the injured person asks you to stay longer, limit the length of visits to about one minute for each day he's been hospitalized; shorter if he seems tired or physically uncomfortable.) Following each visit, ask your child to tell you about what he saw and heard and felt in the room. Be generous with your own story, describing what you've learned about people in pain and how you learned it—including mistakes and discomfort, if that's part of your real story. In the event of an extended recuperation, help your child figure out how to remain appropriately engaged without either hovering over or abandoning his friend.

- Help your youngster work through blame by examining responsibility. Doing stupid stuff isn't evil; it's just stupid. But that doesn't make the pain go away. An accident that occurred under the influence of alcohol wasn't really an accident; it was a dumb—possibly criminal—act by someone who knew better and did it anyway. (What we know isn't as important as how we behave.)

- Reassure your child of God's kindness and patience. Be present with her through the ordeal of grief. Assure her it's okay to still be alive. Encourage her to live with purpose.

- Open up the realities of cause and effect in the physics of life. Few cars and even fewer drivers can take a 30 miles-an-hour curve at 60 miles an hour. Fatigue increases the likelihood of errors in judgment.

- Help your teenager work through forgiveness by exploring the continuum of apologies, amends, restitution, and changed behavior.

- Help your adolescent deconstruct the Myth of Invincibility: *Accidents happen to other people.* Help him discover that no one is smart (or strong or blessed or lucky) enough to be exempt from accidents.

- Gently resist the narcissist who wants to make everything about her: *I wonder what God is trying to teach me through this.* Affirm the sober truth that God causes the sun to rise on the evil and the good and sends rain on the righteous and the unrighteous and sometimes things— good and bad—happen for no apparent reason.

- Watch for signs of self-medication, self-injurious behavior, and bingeing in your child and in her friends.

- Be a champion of mercy. Offer to mediate in relationships broken by an accident.

- Strike a sane tone about accidents. For example, if your child is (or hopes to be) a licensed driver, say something like, "Look, sooner or later, you're going to have an accident in the car. I know this because it happens to everyone. I'm counting on you to do everything in your power to make sure that when it happens, it's minor. Is that fair?" Then when it happens, remember what you said.

4.2 ANGER

Most of the time the story behind the story of anger is fear.

- Fear of failure

- Fear of being victimized

- Fear of losing control

- Fear of looking bad or losing face

- Fear of missing out

- Fear of being wrong

- Fear of being disrespected

- Fear of abandonment, pain, or death

Fear doesn't do much to improve a teenager's quality of life but it doesn't usually get kids in trouble. *Anger* does. Angry kids break things, scratch, steal, and deface things. They harm people and animals. They injure themselves. Angry kids argue and brawl and use baseball bats and automobiles and their own strength as weapons. And sometimes angry adolescents use *weapons* as weapons. All these behaviors stretch along a crisis continuum from fuming to tantrums to rage to terminally lethal behavior.

ACTION PLAN: ESTABLISH LINKAGES

In most anger crises—the ones that don't involve crimes—you can intervene (and maybe even prevent further crisis) by helping your child link his angry behavior to the underlying fear.

That does not mean an angry interrogation where you demand, "What is *wrong* with you? What are you afraid of?" It means getting face-to-face, asking questions, and deep listening. The stories that emerge will help you and your kid link the anger to the underlying fear. Is your daughter afraid of failing? Help her figure out why. Is she afraid of losing control? Help her discover the source of that fear. Whatever she's afraid of, help her get to the bottom of it and figure out a way to live through the fear and redirect her anger into creative action.

If your teenager crosses the line into legal trouble, your access becomes more difficult and the stakes are higher. Don't count on the juvenile justice system to help your son resolve his anger—it could happen but don't count on it. If your child's behavior lands him in the legal system, do everything you can to help him with the same kind of deep listening you would employ under less severe constraints.

Finding out if *your* behavior is the source of your child's anger may be as easy as asking; but probably not. Bring in a third party—if things aren't too bad, consider a skilled youth worker before you turn to a therapist—to help you get the truth about that.

Whatever you do, please don't check out. Sustained engagement is the key to breaking through anger. When a teenager converts anger to proactive, creative behavior she has a fighting chance at moving beyond her sense of helplessness to a growing experience of personal capability where she generates real change instead of just doling out punishment.

4.3 BULLYING

Bullying and hazing have a great deal to do with anger—and entitlement. Despite the old clichés about low self-esteem, research shows that bullies tend to have a relatively high opinion of themselves.

The best data we have identifies five parties to bullying:[1]

- Bullies

- Victims

- Bully/Victims

- Bystanders

- Inattentive Adults

BULLIES

Seven to 13 percent of schoolchildren bully others but are not bullied themselves.

Compared to non-bullying peers, most bullies—

- Have an inflated opinion of themselves

- Enjoy high social status

- Experience high levels of avoidance by peers

- Want to be the center of attention

- Have trouble taking criticism

- Are more likely to abuse alcohol and other drugs

- Are at greater risk of being victimized themselves (about half become victims at some point)

- Are more likely to express conduct disorder, attention deficit-hyperactivity disorder, and other mental health problems

- Are more likely to carry a weapon in and out of school (43.1 percent and 52.2 percent)

- Are more likely to fight frequently and be injured in fights (38.7 percent and 45.7 percent)

- Are more likely to display antisocial and criminal behavior in adulthood

VICTIMS

About 10 percent of children attending school are bullied but don't bully others. Compared to non-victims, bullying victims—

- Are at greater risk for physical and mental health problems such as stomachaches, headaches, and depression

- Miss school more frequently because of fear

- Experience higher levels of anxiety into adulthood

- Struggle with feelings of low self-worth

- Express high levels of depression, social anxiety, and loneliness

- Experience high levels of avoidance by peers

- Have low social status

- Have few friends (it's unclear whether they tend to be victims because they have few friends or have few friends because they're victims)

- Feel that control of their lives is in others' hands

BULLY/VICTIMS

About 6% of schoolchildren both bully and are bullied at school.

Compared to their classmates, bully/victims—

- Have higher levels of conduct and school problems

- Are less engaged in school

- Report high levels of depression and loneliness

- Experience the highest levels of avoidance by peers

BYSTANDERS

About three quarters of schoolkids are not bullies nor are they bullied. About 22 percent live along the margins of bullying, where they observe the behavior without being substantially drawn in.

INATTENTIVE ADULTS

Bullying requires motive and opportunity. Adult intervention narrows the range of opportunities. Taken a step farther, benevolent attentive adults reduce the motivation to bully, which appears to be otherwise self-sustaining among children.

ACTION PLAN: PAY ATTENTION

You can play a crucial role in curtailing bullying by paying attention to your own child's behavior and insisting that the adults who run schools, church groups, and youth organizations do the same.

- Be clear about what you mean when you talk about bullying:

    - Hitting, slapping, kicking, pushing, tripping, spitting, or otherwise assaulting another person is bullying.

    - Name-calling, unrelenting teasing, ethnic, sexual, racial or body-type insults—whether in person, on the Internet, via mobile phone or in written form—is bullying.

    - Threatening, menacing, cursing, or otherwise verbally attacking—whether in person, on the Internet, via mobile phone or in written form—is bullying.

    - Theft or intentional damage to property belonging to another person is bullying.

    - Insulting or threatening notes, e-mails, text messages, graffiti, instant messages, or other forms of communication meant to harm another person is bullying.

    - Spreading rumors about, marginalizing, excluding, or otherwise intimidating another person socially or psychologically—whether in person, on the Internet, via mobile phone, or in written form—is bullying.

- Be one of those benevolent, attentive adults who reduce the motivation for bullying by engaging your child in transformational experiences. In a better world, parents would prevent bullying simply by parenting. We don't live in that world, so watch and listen to find out who may be a bully. (Remember the percentages: If your child is in a classroom with 30 kids, he may easily know two habitual bullies.)

- Don't let bullying in any form whatsoever go unchallenged in your relational web. None. Healthy parents teach their children to care for the poor, the weak, the blind, the lame, and the sick—just the kind of people bullies target. So don't allow anyone (ANYONE!) to harm the weak while you stand by and watch.

- Pay special attention to middle schoolers. Bullying festers in sixth through eighth grade.

- If you find out someone you know is a bullying victim, intervene on her behalf—including appropriate engagements with school personnel, other parents, and law enforcement. (Again, remember the percentages; if your child is in a class with 30 students, she could easily know two habitual victims.)

- Bullies enjoy unaccountable levels of social status at school. Other kids fear and hate and avoid bullies, but for some reason they don't strip them of their social power. Even—perhaps *especially*—if your kid is not a bullying victim, encourage her to mobilize the 20 or more+ percent of student bystanders who regularly witness bullying to denounce such behavior as childish, troubled, and surprising from someone who people seem to think is cool. When the 20 percent stand up, there's a good chance the other 50+ percent will back them on it.

- Encourage school personnel and other adults who work with kids to take an annual survey on bullying as a jumping-off point for group learning and decision making about what behaviors will be tolerated by the peer group.

- Engage your child in developing a sophisticated emotional vocabulary so he can express himself with vivid clarity and depth across a broad range of human experience. (See section 5.1 in this book.)

- Mobilize other adults. If the athletic teams in your community have evolved a culture of bullying, address that with other parents, teachers, administrators, coaches, youth workers, and your child's friends (especially athletes). If you know a youth worker, suggest that he offer to develop content for team meetings, classroom sessions, parent meetings, and school assemblies on making your community a bully-free zone. The material in this book and in *The Youth Worker's Guide to Helping Teenagers in Crisis* (Zondervan|Youth Specialties, 2005) is a good starting place.

- Check yourself. Could anyone argue convincingly that you've bullied retailers, employees, neighbors, friends, kids, other parents, or your significant other? If so, do whatever it takes to make amends and get that turned around.

4.4 CHEATING

Some students start cheating because they're overwhelmed; others start because they're under-challenged.

The overwhelmed student probably starts cheating to save face or, oddly, to please parents who have let him know how important grades are but may not have told him they value *learning* even more. If grades matter more than learning, cheating may offer back-door access to what he wants in the classroom and at home—until the deception unravels.

The under-challenged student may begin cheating because she's bored and distracted. It's possible she's not so much under-challenged as *unengaged* compared to other learning experiences where she can't seem to get enough. In either case, the problem is not that she can't do the work but that she doesn't care to.

It's probably a mistake to assume that either the overwhelmed or the under-challenged student starts cheating because he's lazy—*unmotivated* perhaps, especially the under-challenged student, and quite possibly *demotivated* by the lack of satisfying outcomes. Find out why a student cheats, and you'll know how to address the problem.

It's worth noting that cheating itself does not generally constitute a crisis. It's getting caught that precipitates the crisis, and *getting caught* is an unintended consequence.

ACTION PLAN: ADDRESS ROOT CAUSES

The overwhelmed student will need extra help, perhaps in the form of tutoring or an accomplished study partner. Find out if he's behind in more than one subject. If so, explore the possibility of deeper or more extensive problems. How is his eyesight? Does he process information effectively, or does he struggle with auditory or visual input? This will require a professional evaluation because kids with lifelong process disabilities—dyslexia for example—probably don't have the language to compare what they see and hear with the capacity enjoyed by most others.

The overwhelmed student may need assurance that his struggle is not a character flaw even if his attempts to cover it up were less than honorable.

The under-challenged student is a different kettle of fish. A student who under-achieves may need to be fast-tracked. This is the kind of thing that must be assessed by educators, assuming your school has that capacity. But that doesn't mean you can't ask the question.

Consider the possibility that the under-challenged cheater is distracted by issues that are invisible to you. Find out what else is going on: Is she in relational flux? Is she being harassed or bullied at school, on the job, in the neighborhood, or at church? Has she experienced a big disappointment? Is she grieving a significant loss (significant to *her*—it doesn't matter if it seems significant to others)? Is she anxious about growing up in general or leaving home in particular?

Two other things: (1) Some students take cheating in stride because so many others do it.

JH: A group of bright, high-achieving students once told me it was really hard to earn a *B* while other students were stealing *A*s. I've heard other students casually admit to cheating on subjects that didn't matter to them. "I wouldn't cheat on something important," they'd say, "but I'm not going to major in geography, so what does it matter?"

Persuading a student that learning is more important than grades may take some doing since, after all, you must first be persuaded of that yourself. Are you? (Tread lightly here; your teenager's crap detector will go off if you try to bluff.)

(2) Cheating can be habit-forming. Some people get quite a rush from cheating—not unlike the buzz others get from shoplifting things they can readily afford to buy or don't actually want. The solution to that kind of thrill seeking has much to do with issues of compulsion and addictive behavior (see section 4.18).

4.5 CUTTING+SELF-INJURIOUS **BEHAVIOR**

Why in the world would anybody cut, burn, scratch, hit, bite, gouge, brand, or carve her body? Or yank out her hair? Or bang her head?

She may be diagnosed with mental retardation, autism, or bipolar disorder. She may suffer depression, anxiety, or post-traumatic stress disorder. She may be a victim of abuse or sexual assault.

Self-injurious behavior (SIB) is repetitive but non-lethal self-injury. An adolescent engaged in SIB can do considerable tissue damage, but he's not attempting slow suicide. In fact people most often engage in SIB as pain management to *keep from killing themselves.* He inflicts physical pain to express emotional and spiritual pain. SIB may be a way to manage fear, rage, emptiness, isolation, and sorrow. Victimized adolescents who lack the capacity to resolve their pain by talking about it may express their agony and depleted self-esteem through self-harming. Eating disorders often coexist with SIB.

GIVE ME A SIGN

- Lots of bracelets stacked at the wrist or ankle

- Razor blades, box cutters, paring knives, open paper clips, or broken glass stashed in their bedroom or among their belongings

- Peeled skin

- Scratched skin

- Patchy hair loss

- Many self-mutilators attack out-of-the-way tissue that no one can see—which may lead them to avoid wearing bathing suits or keeping medical appointments

- Most adolescents will continue self-injurious behavior until the underlying problem is resolved—right into adulthood. Medication may alleviate symptoms of anxiety, stress, or depression, but the main treatment for self-mutilation is uncovering and addressing the root cause(s) of the pain

ACTION PLAN: OPENNESS

- Acknowledge that you know about cutting and other forms of SIB and that you aren't shocked to learn that people try to manage their pain that way.

- Don't confuse SIB with moderate body piercing or tattooing. *Excessive* piercing or tattooing is worth looking into.

- If you know (or even suspect) that your child suffered assault, sexual abuse, or some other trauma, don't hesitate to ask gently but directly if she ever feels like hurting herself in times of high stress. If you get a *yes* or a soft *no*, then ask directly if she's done anything to hurt herself. Don't be afraid to ask if she was ever assaulted, sexually abused, or had some other traumatic experience if you're not sure.

- Same thing if you see signs that may indicate self-injury: Ask gently and directly if the injury is what it looks like. If you don't buy the response, press for a clearer answer.

- If you believe that apparent SIB damage is a botched suicide, see sections 2.2 (SLAP) and 4.19 (Suicide).

- By all means, if you feel as though you're in over your head, call in professional reinforcements sooner rather than later (see section 3.1).

- Teach a child who expresses SIB a richer emotional vocabulary (see section 5.1 and appendix 6.3).

- Encourage journaling, writing poetry, drawing, making music, and filmmaking.

- Teach coping tactics such as—

  - Seeking companionship rather than isolating

  - Meditating on *The Serenity Prayer* (appendix 6.6)

  - Practicing self-distraction techniques (for instance, short bursts of exercise or controlled breathing)

- Help your child keep working on the underlying causes until they're resolved.

- Be aware that some kids are tempted to return to self-injurious behavior the next time life gets out of balance... and the next. Be prepared to return to the top of this list and go again.

4.6 DEATH

You may be called on to tell your child that a loved one or close friend has died. If so—

- Try to share the news in person. Don't use the telephone unless you have no other choice. If you're too far away to share the news in person, then consider other flesh-and-blood options such as a kind person who has a relationship with your child.

- Outline the basic facts in a straightforward manner. The gravity of your message probably will be communicated in your demeanor long before any words are spoken. Beyond the basics, provide details as they're requested.

- It will take time for the reality of what you've communicated to sink in. Recognize that kids respond to tragedy in many different ways: shock, tears, silence, anger, blame, disbelief, withdrawal...

- After you've shared the news, stay with your child until you feel confident she's able to function. If you must leave before you feel that confidence, ask another caregiver to remain with her.

- Be sensitive to the need for privacy. Test your sense about that by excusing yourself for a few minutes at a time.

- Make it difficult to isolate or self-medicate. The latter may be challenging if there are adults around who drown their sorrows or otherwise numb their feelings.

- Make it clear that it's acceptable—important even—to take meals, to sleep, to get fresh air, to be in the moment. Review the attributes of a helper in section 2.3.

ACTION PLAN: PREPARE ADOLESCENTS FOR DEATH

We live in a death-denying culture. Prepare your teenager to face death by:

- Talking plainly about mortality

- Taking your child to funerals and talking about the experience afterward

- Allowing your child to accompany you when you visit grieving friends and family—including a funeral home viewing, if that's part of your custom. Without being morbid, welcome questions and demythologize any misconceptions about the processes attached to burial and cremation.

- Talking about what you believe happens in the aftermath of death.

Stages of Grief

Teach the five stages of grief articulated by the psychiatrist and writer Elisabeth Kübler-Ross: *Denial, Anger, Bargaining, Depression,* and *Acceptance.*[1] Preparing your children to grieve with those who grieve also prepares them for their own inevitable grief.

DENIAL. A common initial response to news of death is to deny the possibility as if we believe our denial will somehow make the loss go away. Funerals and memorial services go a long way toward finalizing the realization that it's really happened.

ANGER. Anger over abandonment; anger at the one who caused premature death; self-directed anger; anger at the dead; anger at God. We are most helpful when we create an environment in which kids have permission to verbalize their anger as a normal part of working through grief.

BARGAINING. Be aware of the attempt by some—especially the young—to bargain with God: *God, if you'll bring back my mommy, I promise never to disobey again.* The hope that they might have even the slightest control over the return of a loved one may be all some kids have to hang onto for a while. You see the impossibility of that, but it takes some time to sink in for a grieving child.

DEPRESSION. The numbness that may protect young people in the beginning of grief can trap them later as the magnitude of the loss sinks in. Part of the problem is the perception that everyone else has moved on and the adolescent is alone in his grief. That's when your attention may be most significant. One way to keep checking in is by inviting recollections along the lines of, *I always think of your father when I hear that song* or *Your brother would be cracking up right now.*

ACCEPTANCE. Acceptance happens when it happens. Though there's still a hole where the lost loved one is supposed to be, it becomes possible to function without him. Bit by bit things get back to normal—or the new normal.

Read the survivor care tips in the section on suicide (4.19) for more ideas on how to care for your grieving child.

4.7 DIVORCE

Divorce shakes you off the ground

Divorce whirls you all around.

Divorce makes you all confused

Divorce forces you to choose.

Divorce makes you feel all sad

Divorce pushes you to be mad.

Divorce makes you wonder who cares

Divorce leaves you thoroughly scared.

Divorce makes a silent home

Divorce leaves you all alone.

Divorce is supposed to be an answer

Divorce, in fact, is emotional cancer.

—10-year-old Chicago girl[1]

IT HAPPENS IN EVERY NEIGHBORHOOD

When Rebecca was just five years old, she startled her mom with a simple but pointed question, "Mommy, when are you and Daddy gonna get a divorce?" Nothing at home had given Becky any cause to believe her parents' marriage was in trouble. No couples in her extended family or in her parents' circle of adult friends were separated, divorced, or even moving in that direction. Still, she assumed it was inevitable. At age five.

It turned out Becky had been watching a television program dedicated to helping kids with divorced parents; it was an episode of *Mr. Rogers' Neighborhood*. And that about covers it. The dissolution of families is an indisputable fact of life. The impact of that falls heavily on children who tend to internalize four kinds of messages: *Humiliation, Guilt, Distrust,* and *Lowered Expectations.*

Humiliation

Imagine being torn between *ex-lovers*. Perhaps you don't have to imagine it. While peers continue with the normal developmental tasks of childhood and adolescence, kids of divorce must contend with the adjustment issues that result from family disruptions:

- Custody—who will live with whom and when and where?

- Emotional upheaval in the custodial parent

- Hostility between parents

- Personal grief

- Financial stress as a result of maintaining two households

- Increased responsibility for day-to-day household operations

- Anger toward parents, dates, and stepparents

- New household rules and roles

Many adolescents are embarrassed to talk about their parents' separation or divorce. Some would rather suffer the agony and loneliness of silence than the risk of ridicule or, worse, being blown off by peers with a been-there-done-that attitude. All this conspires to undermine a child's sense of balance. The result is an unpredictable mix of dispositions that can range from shame to blame.

Guilt

Lots of teenagers feel responsible for their parents' divorce—even if it happened when they were children. They struggle with self-doubt, wondering what they did to cause it or what they could have done to prevent it. In rehearsing the past, they construct scenarios where the fingers of blame point back in their direction. In thinking about the future, they concoct schemes to bring their parents back together again.

In families where the announcement of divorce comes as a total shock, children are more apt to assume personal responsibility than in families where war raged and sides were clearly drawn. In the latter case, children may feel guilty if they're relieved by the cessation of open hostilities.

Parents who wait until the last minute to tell children about their intention to separate or divorce minimize the opportunity for kids to process what's going on. Children need to ask important questions (*Will we still see you? Do you still like us?*) and receive vital assurances from *both* parents (*We still love you. This has nothing to do with your behavior. It's between us.*). Without that unpleasant but important processing, the likelihood that children will own responsibility for the separation increases significantly, making their adjustment that much more difficult.

Distrust

You know the old adage: *Fool me once, shame on you; fool me twice, shame on me.* Kids who endure divorce risk losing faith in adults.

In an attempt to justify their actions, the adult (one is all it takes) may share grisly details that make the other parent look bad, irresponsible, and irredeemably at fault. The games angry parents play are further compounded by relatives and friends interested in convincing the children who's really the bad guy. The courts—whose mission is to *protect* the interests of children—often draw kids into an arena where they're used by one parent against the other.

When the smoke clears, kids are left wondering if there's *anyone* they can trust. Author David Elkind:

> Consider for a moment what divorce does to adolescents' sense of parental wisdom, competence, and values. This event not only confronts adolescents with difficult problems of self-definition, but it also changes their perceptions of adult authority. Many teenagers think, for example, that because their parents have messed up their own lives, they have nothing to teach the young adolescent about life and love. And when, in some single-parent homes, teenagers are treated as total equals to the remaining parent, this also contributes to the decline of parental authority. (Such equal treatment is particularly perilous in early adolescence, when young people badly need the guidance and limit-setting of a more knowledgeable adult.)[2]

Lowered Expectations

It's not unusual to hear teenagers from disrupted families express the conviction that they'll never enjoy a happy marriage—or the opinion that there's no such thing.

ACTION PLAN: REALISTIC HOPE

- Even if your marriage doesn't survive, expose your kids to realistically healthy relational models. Relate to teenagers in ways that teach problem solving, sympathy, empathy, negotiation, conflict resolution, forgiveness, and restoration.

- Help your children understand the limits of adulthood. Deconstruct the myths of adult omnipotence and omni-competence. (This isn't that hard; they're already waking up to the fact that their parents are as goofy as anybody else—the trick is helping kids learn to become generous instead of cynical.)

- Ask stable and caring adult family members and friends to come alongside your children as soon as possible after you separate. Investigative reporter Warner Troyer interviewed hundreds of American and Canadian children, youth, and adults who were children of divorce. "The most essential insight," Troyer observes, "is simply that parents, after divorce, aren't all that great. Other adult company and friendship is needed."[3]

- Get yourself to a reputable divorce recovery group— preferably with an adolescent component for your child. Request that your former spouse engage such a group as well.

- Don't cling but don't forget to extend appropriate expressions of affection when kids are going through divorce. The experience of wholesome touch can be scarce during family blow-ups, but remember that affection must be welcome to be appropriate.

- Don't hesitate to call in reinforcements for a chronically depressed teenager.

- Remember the flight attendant's speech: *In the event of a cabin depressurization, a mask will drop from the panel above you. Secure your own mask first; then help your child with his mask.* It really is important to get your own mask in place because you'll be no good to anyone if you pass out while trying to assist them. That said, don't take so long that your youngster turns blue waiting for help.

4.8 DROPPING **OUT**

Kids who drop out of school tend to be underemployed: Dropouts faced 48 percent unemployment at the turn of the twenty-first century (66 percent for black males). And those who worked earned only 65 percent of the U.S. median income—meaning they earned 35 percent less than a middle-income worker.[1] Among black Americans, a male who drops out of high school is 60 times more likely to go to prison than one with a bachelor's degree (the one with the degree will also, by the way, enjoy lifetime earnings more than double those of a high school graduate—a difference of more than a million dollars).[2] It's increasingly clear that most teenagers don't drop out of school for the money.

ACTION PLAN: CUT TO THE CHASE

- Find out what's behind a kid's intention to drop out of school. The presenting problem is seldom the root cause. Address what's not obvious. Look for—

  - Anxiety about growing up or unfinished childhood business

  - Hidden addictions

  - Victimization at school

  - Learning disabilities

  - Extraordinary untapped ability

- Pregnancy

- Income from illegal activities

- Relational conflict

If you learn that school isn't really the issue, then dropping out won't fix what's wrong. Help your child identify and solve the real problem.

- If school really is the problem then recommend appropriate alternatives. For some students a high school equivalency certificate is as good as—or better than—walking at graduation with a class of peers they care little about. For students utterly de-motivated by the high school experience or profoundly motivated by another pursuit for which they show aptitude, suggest a General Education Degree (GED) or High School Equivalency program. It's the learning (or at least the certificate) that matters, not the stereotypical high school experience. Suspend your preconceptions and take a clearheaded look at what will move your child forward in life. If it's a GED or High School Equivalency test, then help the kid prepare to pass the test and get on with his life.

- Do what you can to help your child find *meaningful* work, where meaning is measured by direct productivity or by income that supports personal growth and service rather than purely disposable income.

- If your child walks an alternative path, help her figure out how to find meaningful peer relationships. Middle-adolescents are seldom served by being thrown into a pool of significantly older people in the workplace or community—not to put too fine a point on it, but your 17-year-old doesn't need to be dating a 23-year-old. So help her find places where she can develop age-appropriate relationships.

- Help your adolescent develop and work toward a desirable scenario for the future. Use the Action Plan Worksheet in appendix 6.1 to help him develop a plan that covers immediate educational concerns; then work through it a second time to develop a plan to get where he wants to go as a creative, productive worker.

4.9 EATING **DISORDERS**

Current science suggests a conspiracy of genetic and behavioral factors behind the startling increase of *obesity* (body weight more than 20 percent higher than recommended for height) and *morbid obesity* (body weight more than 100 pounds over the recommended weight for height) in the United States. U.S. census data shows an increase in the number of overweight children and adolescents from about six percent in 1980 to 18 percent at this writing.[1] In our opinion this has much to do with the use of food as a mood-altering substance.

At the other end of the food chain are the eating disorders known as *anorexia nervosa* and *bulimia nervosa*.

The *anorexic* suffers from extreme weight loss related to emotional, not physiological, difficulties. Complex spiritual, emotional, and social interactions combine with a twisted body image to make any weight gain abhorrent. Translated, *anorexia nervosa* means *nervous loss of appetite.*

Bulimia is a condition characterized by binge eating—consuming incredibly large quantities of food in a short period of time—after which the eater induces vomiting or abuses laxatives in order to purge the food. The term *bulimia* is derived from a compound Greek word meaning *ox-hunger* (as in, *hungry as an ox*). So *bulimia nervosa* translates roughly as *nervous hunger.*

The majority of anorexics and bulimics are middle- and upper-middle-income females. Obesity is an equal-opportunity employer. The onset of anorexia and bulimia tends to happen near puberty, but its roots may go much deeper into childhood body image issues. Puberty may be an activator (among several triggers) as the thickening and curving of the female form raises fears about fatness, leaving childhood, performing in adult contexts, failure, loss of control, sexuality, and generalized angst.

GIVE ME A SIGN

In *Walking a Thin Line*, Pam Vredevelt and Joyce Whitman identify key characteristics of anorexia and bulimia.[2]

Anorexia Nervosa

- Voluntary starvation often leading to emaciation and sometimes death
- Occasional binges, followed by fasting, laxative abuse, or self-induced starvation
- Menstrual period ceases or may not begin if anorexia occurs before puberty
- Excessive exercise
- Hands, feet, and other parts of the body are always cold
- Dry skin
- Head hair may thin, but downy fuzz can appear on other parts of the body
- Depression, irritability, deceitfulness, guilt, and self-loathing
- Thinks, *I'm much too fat*, even when emaciated
- Obsessive interest in food, recipes, and cooking
- Rituals involving food, exercise, and other aspects of life
- Perfectionist
- Introverted and withdrawn
- Avoids people
- Maintains rigid control

Bulimia Nervosa

- Secretive binge eating—can occur regularly and may follow a pattern (caloric intake during a binge can range from 1,000 to 20,000 calories)
- Binges are followed by fasting, laxative abuse, self-induced vomiting, or other forms of purging (or person may chew food but spits it out before swallowing)
- Menstrual periods may be regular, irregular, or absent
- Swollen neck glands
- Cavities and loss of tooth enamel
- Broken blood vessels in face
- Bags under the eyes
- Fainting spells
- Rapid or irregular heartbeat
- Miscellaneous stomach and intestinal discomforts and problems
- Weight may often fluctuate because of alternating periods of binges and fasts
- Wants relationships and the approval of others
- Loses control and fears she cannot stop once she begins eating

Add to those characteristics these hints of the presence of anorexia and bulimia:

Anorexia Nervosa	*Bulimia Nervosa*
• Looks not just lean, but abnormally thin • Extreme attraction/avoidance language and behavior regarding food • Obsessive weighing throughout the day • Baggy clothing to hide body shape	• Abnormally frequent trips to the bathroom • Abnormal fixation on exercise, no matter what • Cuts and calluses on knuckles and backs of hands • Car, clothing, or closet smells of vomit

ACTION PLAN: ENGAGE

- Teach your child about eating disorders. Your reasoning: It's damaging behavior that is dangerous and can be deadly.

- If you have food issues, identify them and take steps to regain your health.

- Teach and model healthy nutrition, including healthy snacks.

- Engage your child in generous, open conversation if you see clustered characteristics and hints of eating disorders.

- If you're certain an unacknowledged eating disorder is controlling your kid's life, consider an *intervention*. (See section 3.3.)

- Get to the story behind the story. If an eating disorder is the presenting problem, the core issue may be:

The Parent's Guide to Helping Teenagers in Crisis

- Sexual threat. There is an uncanny coincidence between eating disorders and sexual abuse. By some accounts, more than 80 percent of women treated for eating disorders self-identify as victims of molestation and sexualized violence. Obesity and starvation may be attempts to desexualize. Bulking may amount to gaining protective strength against further abuse. Deal with the sexual abuse, and the eating tends to take care of itself.

- Fear of fatness. Some children have been hammered about their weight to the point of obsession. Deal with self-image and self-esteem needs.

- Fear of leaving childhood. Some children find adolescence threatening. Find out why.

- Fear of performing in adult contexts. Some children are intimidated by adult expectations. Find out why and seek to relieve the pressure.

- Fear of failure. There's a high incidence of *perfectionism* among anorexics and *people pleasing* among bulimics. Find out the meaning a young person assigns to failure and why.

- Loss of control. Some anorexics and obese adolescents are staking out a personal space where a despised and feared adult cannot go: *They can push me around all they want, but they can't control what I eat.* Find out why a kid feels bullied, impotent, or out of control and help her deal with that.

- Generalized angst. Many teenagers have experiences and perceptions of the world that make them anxious and afraid to take responsibility. Food is an amazing, cheap, and legal mood-altering substance. This is food as self-medication. Like the abuse of alcohol and other drugs, kids wouldn't do it if it didn't work. Find out why the child is afraid and help him tackle and overcome his fear (see section 4.18).

- Don't hesitate to call in reinforcements when you believe you're in over your head. That said, there are no miracles in treatment, and many teenagers bluff their way through counseling relationships and treatment programs. So—

  - Plan to be in it for the long haul. Everybody has to face food pretty much every day. Thus, the presenting problem can never be isolated from normal life. The recovering food addict needs to know you understand the struggle.

  - Push through your fear (likely mixed with frustration expressed as anger) and learn as much as you can about eating disorders. Don't flinch. Eating disorders frequently include a family component that lies beneath the presenting problem. That means solving food issues often requires addressing family issues.

  - Embrace your suffering child with grace, sensitivity, firm resolve, and the knowledge that the fix takes time.

4.10 HAZING

JH: There was an angry ritual at my high school—it had been going on as long as anyone could recall. On the last day of football practice (the day before the last game of the season), once the coaches left the field, the seniors lined up between the goalposts and made the younger boys pass through them. I suppose it was the seniors' last chance to express their *appreciation* for their teammates.

As a sophomore I watched older guys beat on younger guys; I remember an enormous kid on top of me, pounding on my face mask, then letting me up without doing much damage. As a junior I got off easy because I was a starter. We'd had a frustrating season, but apparently none of the seniors was too frustrated with me.

Things were different on the last day of practice in 12th grade. That year our final game would be for the state championship. In 24 hours we'd be in the Florida State University Seminoles' locker room preparing to go before a capacity crowd and win or lose the state title.

Before that final practice, there was a brief discussion among the seniors about the value of tradition. As the tide turned from tradition toward teamwork, a couple of guys expressed frustration that they wouldn't have the chance to do to someone else what was done to them. Ultimately though, no one wanted revenge more than he wanted a state championship. When the coaches left us alone on the field that day, we called the team into a huge huddle, churned the worn-out sod with our cleats, hollered, cheered, and mainlined adrenaline like the junkies we were. The scrum ended with a mighty shout, and we all ran through the goalposts together.

As far as I know, the goalpost beating tradition died that afternoon. The next day we won the state title.

I don't know that organized sports are inherently flawed, but I think *people* are. The anger many of us felt in those days didn't just go away because we chose not to beat up our younger teammates. It went somewhere else. I'm just glad we didn't generate even more anger for those younger guys.

Unfortunately, this is a culture in which we victimize others on a regular basis. We do the things that were done to us—the things that made us angry and crazy—and then our victims do those things too. It just about never ends until somebody swims against the tide just enough to ask, "Is this gonna help us win the state championship? Because if it isn't, I don't think we should do it."

Hazing is a strange, shame-based ritual in which strong (or privileged) people humiliate weak (or newly arrived) people in order to initiate them into a closed society. And isn't it fascinating that the privilege of membership includes inflicting pain on those who follow?

How is hazing supposed to make us better people? It's not. It's supposed to make us loyal. It's supposed to make us compliant so we're willing to take whatever's next; so we're ready to take one for the team.

Of high school students who say they wouldn't report hazing, 24 percent agree with the statement: "Other kids would make my life miserable." Sixteen percent agree with the statement: "I just wouldn't tell on my friends, no matter what."[1]

ACTION PLAN: BUILD BETTER RITUALS

As in the case of organized sports, it's not the *idea* of initiation that's broken; it's the people doing the initiating. We don't have to throw out the idea, just redeem it. Done right, initiation is a valuable rite of passage that celebrates progress by letting young people in on the secrets of their human and spiritual communities.

> **JH:** I went to work for a church that had a tradition of kidnapping the new ninth-grade class on a Saturday morning—it was their way of initiating freshmen into the high school group. Students with driver's licenses were dispatched with a couple of partners to fetch the young ones from their beds while it was still dark. Some of the older kids liked to wear camo and face paint and use a little duct tape as part of the kidnapping. Of course, the parents were in on the gag and sworn to silence. It was a blast.
>
> Well, it was a blast as long as you weren't one of the abductees, who tended to be disoriented by the experience, sometimes a bit roughed up, and almost universally embarrassed (except for those girls who were tipped off by an older friend and sat fully dressed and made up, waiting for the kidnappers to arrive—for them it probably worked out all right). Asking around a bit, I heard enough stories of unpleasantness to understand why that was the first and last time some students came to the senior high group.
>
> So I stopped it. I figured there must be a better way to welcome the incoming class than humiliating and scaring them half to death. A few older kids complained for about 30 seconds before admitting it never seemed quite right to them either and we got on with inventing some new rituals.

Effective initiations build relationships and a growing sense of belonging based on mutual respect and sharing. Any ritual that violates that spirit endangers the mission of the organization because it endangers the well-being of participants.

4.11 Hazing + 127

- Don't cause your children to endure humiliating experiences in order to be accepted by adults in your family.

- Engage adults in your community to end hazing in schools, sports teams, and youth organizations.

- Gather a group of mature students and adults and brainstorm a continuum of honoring, engaging rituals to initiate newcomers and involve old-timers in passing on community culture. Armed with those examples, encourage organizations in your community to develop more creative ways of initiating younger students as they grow up.

- Create something insanely counterintuitive, like a day on which seniors compete to outdo each other by serving the freshmen.

4.11 **INCEST**

No one wants to believe any adult relative would sexually victimize a kid.

According to the most widely regarded research we know, about 16 percent of women are sexually abused by a relative before age 18.[1] That's about one girl in six. A literature review suggests about half as many boys are incest victims, but it's widely thought that sexual abuse of boys is underreported and the number may be higher.[2] Taking it as it lies, that means there's a possibility that one in six girls and one in 12 boys you know is at risk from someone you both should be able to trust.

The stakes are high. It won't be hard for you to imagine the difficulty of disclosing a sexualized relationship with a family member. Most incest situations involve father-daughter or stepfather-stepdaughter relationships. Mother-son or stepmother-stepson incidents are much less common—when they do occur, they're even more damaging and difficult to treat.

A study reported by the New York City Alliance Against Sexual Abuse estimates that 60 percent of women and 25 percent of men who reported childhood victimization by their mothers have eating disorders. Eighty percent of the women and all the men reported sexual problems as adults. Almost two-thirds of the women said examinations by doctors or dentists were terrifying.

Other studies referenced by the Alliance report a higher incidence among incest survivors of intense guilt and shame, low self-esteem, depression, substance abuse, sexual promiscuity, and post-traumatic stress disorder—with symptoms of flashbacks, nightmares, and amnesia—than among people assaulted by strangers.[3]

Because it is so terribly difficult to admit that a father, uncle, brother, or other family member finds them sexually attractive—or inconceivably wants to dominate them—and has acted on those impulses, most child and adolescent victims live in what some have come to call *silent shame*.

ACTION PLAN: LISTEN

- Admitting incest is an act of (sometimes desperate) trust. Don't fail to acknowledge the courage that involves. Promise to help the victim and follow through on the promise. Victims of incest need to know that their victimization can and will end.

- Teenagers are more likely to tell a peer than an adult about an incestuous relationship. You probably can't change that, but you may be able to make it work for you. If you communicate openness, sensitivity, and compassion on the subject of incest victims (along with a measured absence of tolerance toward perpetrators), there's a fair chance that a caring sibling, cousin, or friend would inform you about incest.

- Be prepared to address sorrow, anger, and abandonment in victims of incest. Not only were they abused by someone who should have protected and nurtured them, but there's also a chance they believe you failed to take action for too long.

- Be prepared to address denial, resistance, and outright hostility from everyone else in the family. Use the definitions of sexual abuse in section 4.15 to qualify the charge.

- Anticipate guilt, shame, and fear in the victim. Many kids are made to feel responsible for incestuous relationships (which by nature abuse the power of the older over the younger). Reassure the victim she's not to blame. No matter what the situation, the adult perpetrator is responsible for what occurred—period.

- Be prepared to address deep-seated confusion if a child experienced any reflexive sexual response from incestuous contact. Help the teenager understand that an involuntary physical response such as penile erection, vaginal lubrication, or even orgasm does not mean he or she "wanted it" or that the contact was welcome or consensual. Reflexive physical response is not a cause for self-blaming.

- Call in reinforcements early—the closer the relationship of the perpetrator to you, the more difficult it will be for you to deal with the crisis. Get help.

- If in doubt ask a *mandated reporter* for advice. In most states, health care providers, mental health care providers, teachers, social workers, daycare providers, and law enforcement personnel are listed among those required to report suspected or known incidents of child abuse. Church-sponsored schools and daycare centers are mandatory reporters. Nearly half the states include members of the clergy specifically (and child and youth work professionals by inference). In another third of the states, *any person*— meaning *every* person—is classified as a mandatory reporter.

- Don't let anything keep you from fulfilling your legal responsibility. In *The Common Secret,* Ruth and Henry Kempe write:

Whatever the background situation, under the laws of *all* our states and most countries abroad, sexual abuse of children is *always* a criminal act (generally a felony); major psychiatric illness in the perpetrator is a relatively uncommon finding in the vast majority of sexual abuse cases, though it may be more common in forcible rape by a sociopathic criminal; and "therapy" deals with only part of the problem.[4]

- Act in the child's best interest. Most states have multi-disciplinary teams and carefully developed policies designed to protect the child's best interests while working to keep families intact, if possible. The standard is to stabilize the health and safety of the most vulnerable first, then look at restoring equilibrium to the family.[5]

- Network with school personnel—who originate a significant percentage of abuse reports by the way. Bring a school administrator or counselor into your confidence to the extent that they'll at least ask teachers and coaches to keep an eye on your child and inform you if they see trouble in the aftermath of disclosing incest. They don't need to know all the details; just enough to know your kid is going through deep waters and may require extra care.

- Be prepared to get temporary housing for one or more family members. The thought of being responsible for the breakup of their family is terrifying to most kids—regardless of the abuse they've suffered. One way to help keep the family intact is temporarily removing the offending family member from the household during the risk assessment and action plan development—sometimes, leaving with the victimized child is a better option. It's generally more difficult to find people who are ready to welcome a perpetrator into their home, but don't assume it's not possible. There are Christian communities willing to care for both victim and accused (who may be at significant risk of self-harm in the aftermath of disclosure).

- Stay close to the victimized child or teenager. Revealing the sordid details of an incestuous relationship is a gruesome ordeal for almost anyone. Traditionally, the first time a victim tells the story is only the first in a

✛

series of examinations and investigative procedures. These days multidisciplinary intervention teams from Child Protective Services are responsible for reducing the trauma children and youth suffer as a result of a crime against them. The CPS team is trained for the legal, psychological, and familial aspects of a thorough investigation. The result is that kids are spared the agony of having to tell their horror story over and over again to a host of different people. But don't depend on that. Do what it takes to remain close for the duration.

- Be alert for the signs of Self-Injurious Behavior (SIB) listed in section 4.5. Once they've told someone about incest it's not unusual for young people to enter a period of high risk for suicide, drug abuse, and other self-destructive behaviors. Surround the victim with loving concern and make it difficult for him or her to isolate from that care.

4.12 POST-TRAUMATIC **STRESS DISORDER**

Post-traumatic stress disorder (PTSD) is an anxiety disorder that sometimes develops in the aftermath of terrifying events in which assault or bodily injury was witnessed, threatened, or occurred to a child. PTSD is not universal, but post-traumatic stress is. Flashbacks, vivid memories, intrusive thoughts and nightmares, emotional numbness or hyper-arousal, sleep disturbances, depression, anxiety, headaches, stomach complaints, dizziness, chest pain, irritability, outbursts of anger, and feelings of intense guilt are all common experiences in the immediate aftermath of trauma. It's when those experiences are intense and persist beyond a month or so that mental health professionals may diagnose PTSD.

JH: About a month ago, I saw my neighbor inadvertently roll his pickup onto my sleeping dog's foreleg. There were a lot of people milling around, and he quickly got the message that he should stop the vehicle. Meanwhile, the dog was terrified and screaming in pain. My eyes met my dog's eyes, and I felt the intensity of her pain as I rushed to comfort her.

It turned out the damage to dog and driver was fairly minor. All's well that ends well. Still, as recently as yesterday I experienced a deep shudder at an unexpected, vivid memory of the panicky look in my dog's eyes when she picked me out of the crowd. That's post-traumatic stress; it's normal and by itself it's not *post-traumatic stress disorder.*

Misery loves company. Full-blown PTSD may be accompanied by addictive and self-destructive behavior, self-doubt, paranoia, psychotic breaks, severe depression, excessive compliance, fear of intimacy, and an enveloping sense of helplessness, hopelessness, and despair.

PTSD can be triggered by a violent personal assault, rape, or mugging; by natural or human-caused disasters or accidents; or by witnessing or participating in military combat. About 30 percent of those who spend time in war zones suffer from PTSD. People who endured childhood abuse or other prior trauma are somewhat more likely to experience PTSD.

Back in the day, it was generally believed that emotional numbness following a trauma was a sign of resilience. The growing suspicion among researchers today is that people who exhibit emotional distance after trauma may be more disposed to PTSD than those who express a fuller range of emotions.[1]

ACTION PLAN: TALK

The good news is that talking about the trauma helps. Since the diagnosis was recognized in the American Psychiatric Association's *Diagnostic and Statistical Manual of Mental Disorders* in 1980, a body of research has established the effectiveness of cognitive-behavioral therapy and group therapy for working through trauma (both of which are talk-based). Medication may help ease related symptoms of depression, anxiety, and sleeplessness, but it's not necessarily indicated for long-term recovery.

Some studies show that sooner is better for talking through the trauma of catastrophic events. Following a hurricane in Hawaii, a study of 12,000 school children found that two years later those who received counseling soon after the storm were doing better than those who didn't get that kind of help.[2]

If you suspect PTSD, start by creating or finding a safe place to talk. Then, as quickly as possible, get your child to a mental health professional who has experience treating people suffering post-traumatic stress. If the incident in question is some kind of mass disaster—whether it's natural or caused by humans—your youngster will almost certainly benefit from talking with other survivors. Do what you can to facilitate that sort of contact in a healthy environment.

4.13 PREGNANCY

At this writing there is less adolescent sexual activity in general, and sexually active adolescents are more likely to use condoms and birth control pills to lessen the risk of pregnancy. All of which is meaningless if your daughter or your son's girlfriend says she's missed her period.

If that happens, take a deep breath, pray for wisdom, and brace yourself for a lengthy, life-changing intervention.

ACTION PLAN: PROTECT AS MANY LIVES AS POSSIBLE

- Don't rush to judgment. Listen deeply.

- Find out why she believes she's pregnant.

- Has she seen a doctor?

- How far along is she?

- How is her health?

- How is she holding up emotionally?

- What is the status of the relationship between the mother- and father-to-be?

Don't panic. If the girl hasn't had a reliable pregnancy test, that's a good next step, followed closely by a medical evaluation, including tests for sexually transmitted diseases. (There's more on this in section 4.17.)

If your son is the father, hold his feet to the fire. He won't be helped if you shield him from the natural and logical consequences of his behavior.

Ask what your daughter or son thinks is the next step. If the young woman is leaning toward abortion, explore her reasons and perceptions about the possible outcomes as directly and matter-of-factly as you can under the circumstances. Unless you're very familiar with this road, don't hesitate to call for guidance from a third party you know and trust.

Assuming the likelihood that you would counsel against abortion, we doubt you'll get what you want by exerting pressure before you've taken considerable time for deep listening. As always, get the story behind the story. To the young woman, abortion may look like the only reasonable alternative—where *reasonable* means sparing her, you, or her sexual partner from extended pain.

At this writing if a girl elects to have an abortion, a dozen states have no parental notification or permission requirements. The rest require that one or both parents be informed 24 to 48 hours before an abortion or the parents must grant their permission in writing.

If your son or daughter is leaning toward marriage, be just as attentive, direct, and matter-of-fact as you would be if you were discussing abortion—and just as quick to call in reinforcements since you'll very likely be in a heightened emotional state yourself. Ditto if the young woman is leaning toward single parenthood.

Take time to privately and carefully reflect on what it would mean to become a custodial grandparent—don't be naive about that possibility.

It's not difficult to do the homework on adoption alternatives. Enter the word *adoption* in Google search and you'll find lots of national organizations that help pregnant girls and women place newborns for adoption at no cost to the mother. If you have access to a church-based youth worker, ask if his crisis network includes resources to advise and provide services for pregnant teens.

Help your youngster develop several scenarios about desirable and undesirable outcomes, including possible paths from here to there. Ask questions that require consideration of positive and negative effects on everyone involved. Acknowledge what's already begun to dawn on everyone—especially the pregnant girl: There's no easy way through this. Every choice has a ripple effect on other choices and on other people's lives. Knowing there is no easy way, help your child protect as many lives as possible.

4.14 RAPE

Rape is a violent crime. Like all violent crimes, the offender leaves physical evidence in the form of DNA and other identifying markers. Capturing that evidence is a key factor in getting a conviction (and since the majority of rapes and sexual assaults are committed by people known to their victims, it won't be difficult to compare samples).

By now everyone knows prosecuting a rape charge isn't quite as simple as it sounds. Even with physical evidence, proving forcible rape can be made difficult by a vigorous legal defense. Timing is everything. Forensic medical documentation of bruises, abrasions, and DNA evidence in the hours immediately following an attack is vital to a strong physical case. And the few hours immediately following a rape are exactly the time when a victim is most likely to be emotionally incapacitated by the trauma.

If the crime goes unreported for just half an hour, it can very easily turn into half a day; every cycle of the clock makes it more difficult for the victim to report.

The effects of rape—especially a rape that is not addressed by the victim—are well known, including isolation, grief, fear, anger, self-doubt, distrust, regret, depression, substance abuse, eating disorders, cutting, sexual recklessness, and adult sexual dysfunction.

ACTION PLAN: BE THERE

- Teach your sons and daughters that forcible sex is never, ever permissible in any form.

- Teach boys to teach *other* boys that forcible sex is unacceptable and criminal.

- Teach girls that forcible sex is a crime no matter who the offender is.

- Teach girls and boys to report sexual crimes immediately. Promise to drop what you're doing and help them get medical attention and report the crime 24\7\365.

- Take the victim of rape to an emergency care unit as soon as possible after the attack. Adolescent rape victims may resist medical attention because many fear the examination will be painful. Acknowledge the potential for discomfort and point downstream to other possible medical issues including the risk of sexually transmitted infections and the possibility of pregnancy. It's unpleasant, but it has to be addressed: *We really need to get you checked out by a doctor right now.*

- Medical personnel are mandatory sex crime reporters in all states. Legal requirements may necessitate additional medical examinations. Stick with your child through every minute of that process. You don't have to talk; you just have to be there.

- Be present in the months that follow. The medical and law enforcement systems have become fairly sensitive to rape victims and witnesses. Many police departments employ women to interview female rape and sexual assault victims. Victim assistance programs work to make court appearances more tolerable. Be present; provide perspective, another set of ears, loving acceptance, and ongoing support through legal depositions, meetings with police, and court appearances.

- As soon as possible, bring in a psychotherapist with experience in sexual assault recovery.

- Consider helping your child connect with a support group of people who have survived rape.

- Be prepared to address deep-seated confusion if a child experienced any reflexive sexual response from the assault. Involuntary penile erection, vaginal lubrication, or even orgasm does not mean he or she "wanted it" or that the assault was welcome or consensual. Reflexive physical response is not a cause for self-blame.

- Prepare to help your child work through lingering fears, spiritual doubt, social anxiety, and confusing emotions. Be there for as long as it takes.

4.15 SEXUAL **ABUSE**

First, the law.

The U.S. Department of Health and Human Services defines sexual abuse on a child as:

> A type of maltreatment that refers to the involvement of the child in sexual activity to provide sexual gratification or financial benefit to the perpetrator, including contacts for sexual purposes, molestation, statutory rape, prostitution, pornography, exposure, incest, or other sexually exploitative activities.[1]

The glossary of the Child Welfare Information Gateway (formerly known as the National Clearinghouse on Child Abuse and Neglect Information) includes additional refinements:

> Sexual Abuse: Inappropriate adolescent or adult sexual behavior with a child. It includes fondling a child's genitals, making the child fondle the adult's genitals, intercourse, incest, rape, sodomy, exhibitionism, sexual exploitation, or exposure to pornography.[2]

Any of these acts committed by a "person responsible for the care of a child...or related to a child," (for example, a parent, guardian, relative, or caregiver such as a youth worker, teacher, sitter, camp counselor, et al.) is classified as sexual abuse. (For more on incest, see section 4.11.) Sexual abuse allegations are investigated under the guidelines of Child Protective Services agencies in each state. In most instances these acts are criminal offenses. Any of these acts perpetrated by someone not acquainted with the child is classified as sexual assault—always a criminal act handled by police and criminal courts.[3]

THREE CATEGORIES OF SEXUAL ABUSE OF CHILDREN

1. Non-touching—voyeurism, exhibitionism, production or purchase of child pornography, exposure to adult sexual activity

2. Touching—molestation, penetration, incest, child pornography

3. Forced or physically violent—rape, sadism, masochism, child pornography

Non-Touching Sexual Abuse

Sexual abuse of children or adolescents is not limited to physical contact.

A *voyeur* may masturbate while secretly viewing children or adolescents. Voyeurs sometimes seek jobs or volunteer positions in daycare centers, schools, camps, church youth programs, after-school programs, and community centers frequented by children or adolescents.

Exhibitionist pedophiles are aroused by the act or memory of exposing their genitals to minors.

Child pornography involves producing or possessing any visual depiction of a minor in sexually explicit conduct as defined by U.S. Code § 2252:

- "Minor" means any person younger than 18 years old

- "Sexually explicit conduct" means actual or simulated—

  - Sexual intercourse, including genital-genital, oral-genital, anal-genital, or oral-anal, whether between persons of the same or opposite sex

  - Bestiality

  - Masturbation

  - Sadistic or masochistic abuse

  - Lascivious exhibition of the genitals or pubic area of any person[4]

Exposure to adult sexual activity includes situations in which children are encouraged, invited, or forced to watch adults engage in sexual activity with other adults or children.

Touching Forms of Sexual Abuse

Molestation includes inappropriate touch; fondling or kissing a child on the breasts or genitals; or enticing or causing a child to touch, fondle, or kiss the breasts or genitals of an adult.

Sexual intercourse, for legal purposes, includes genital-genital, oral-genital, anal-genital, or oral-anal, whether between persons of the same or opposite sex.

Even in the absence of physical force, sexual intercourse by an adult with a child is classified as *statutory rape.* Different states have slight variations in the age at which legal minors may consent to sexual intercourse. Most states set the age of consent at 18. At this writing, the age of consent is 16 in a few states; and 14 or 15 in a couple of others.

Incest is sexual activity that occurs between family members. In most sexual abuse cases involving children up to the age of 12, the perpetrator is someone who is known, perhaps trusted, and often related to the child as a parent, sibling, grandparent, stepparent, uncle, cousin, or other family member.

Forced or Physically Violent Sexual Assault

Rape is forced sexual intercourse or attempted sexual intercourse committed against a woman, man, girl, or boy against the victim's will and without consent. Before the law, there is no such thing as consensual sex between a legal adult and a legal child—the act always constitutes statutory rape. (For more on helping rape victims, see section 4.14.)

The sadist takes pleasure from and receives sexual stimulation by inflicting pain on another person. Masochists are stimulated by having pain inflicted on them. Sadistic or masochistic incidents are rare in child sexual abuse.

Pedophilia

Pedophiles are predominantly males for whom prepubescent children are objects of sexual desire. Such attractions are not a matter of law unless the adult behaves in a sexualized way toward a minor. Pedophilia may have more to do with age issues than gender *per se*, as pedophiles may commit same-sex, opposite-sex, or either-sex acts on children. The incidence of adult female pedophilia is low but not unheard of.

An infrequently used term for an adult who demonstrates a sexually predatory appetite toward adolescent boys is *pederast*. The behavior is called *pederasty*. There is no corresponding term for those who demonstrate a sexually predatory appetite toward teenage girls—not surprising given the almost universally predatory attitude toward adolescent females in this culture. The closest thing may be "Lolita Syndrome," borrowed from the 1958 Nabokov novel, *Lolita*. Or you could go with *lecher* or *dirty old man*.

ACTION PLAN: EYES WIDE OPEN

- There is no known method by which pedophiles, peder-asts, or lechers can be screened prior to their apprehension for child abuse. So teach your children and adolescents to recognize signs of sexual advance, including inappropriate touching, embracing, and kissing.

- Teach your children and adolescents to recognize signs of seduction, including pleasurable touching, embracing, kissing, and inappropriate gifts and bribes in the form of gifts, special privileges, or favored-child status.

- Teach your children and adolescents enough to understand how and why seduction works. This is important even if a child proves unable to avoid sexual abuse. One factor in post-abuse resilience among boys is a level of sexual knowledge that contextualizes any pleasure response to the abuse so as to reduce the incidence of crippling guilt.[5]

- Be prepared to address confusion if your child experienced any reflexive sexual response from a seductive sexual contact. A physical response such as penile erection, vaginal lubrication, or even orgasm may be involuntary and reflexive and does not mean the contact was welcome or consensual. Reflexive physical response is not a cause for self-blame.

- Teach verbal refusal skills.

- Devise an exit strategy by which your child is empowered to flee a self-defined threat and enabled to get to a safe place to meet you or another trusted adult.

- Teach your children and adolescents to call 911 and tell the dispatcher an older person is threatening them sexually.

- Teach your children and adolescents to report sexual abuse no matter what.

- Pay special attention to preschool boys. According to Department of Justice statistics, boys are most vulnerable to sexual assault at age four.[6]

- Pay special attention to eighth and ninth grade girls. According to Department of Justice statistics, girls are most vulnerable to sexual assault at age 14.[7]

- Insist on a check for prior sex offense convictions for all staff and volunteers who work with children and youth in sports teams, youth groups, and community organizations. The National Sex Offender Registry Web site is at http://www.fbi.gov/hq/cid/cac/registry.htm. All 50 states and the District of Columbia maintain searchable sex offender registries. A list of the state sex offender registries is in appendix 6.5. If you need assistance, local law enforcement officials will help you find out if a person has been convicted of a sex crime.

- All that said, do everything in a way that is evenhanded and human. Nobody needs to feel as though he's on trial because he expresses a desire to help kids grow up whole and healthy. No parent needs to feel her children are at greater risk than they are. No child needs to experience undue suspicion or anxiety about people who truly care for her. Encourage the organizations with which your children interact to practice due diligence before they place adults in contact with kids and to always balance trust and supervision.

- Encourage the leaders of youth organizations to inform parents of their selection process for staff and volunteers who lead children and adolescents, including training, supervision, and evaluation. If you're not satisfied with the level of disclosure, encourage them to train staff and volunteers with clear standards about how and under what circumstances they may demonstrate affection toward children and adolescents (and inform parents of these standards). It's not necessary or desirable to enact a blanket prohibition on appropriate touch. A hand on the shoulder, side-by-side (not pelvic) hugging, tousled hair, and noogies are usually appropriate if the younger person welcomes them. No touch is appropriate if it's unwelcome.

- Urge leaders to train staff and volunteers to recognize signs of sexual abuse in children, beginning with undue displays of physical affection and physical clinging by the child.

- Communicate to your children that you'll be attentive and receptive to sexual abuse disclosures from them. Be aware of factors that make it difficult for your child to inform you about sexual abuse: The age of the child, the relationship with the perpetrator, threats, bribes, how the incident is perceived by the minor, the level of trauma, and the level of trust between you and your child. Kids are more likely to talk about sexual abuse when they're confident of their parents' unconditional love. Parents who don't want to hear bad news usually don't—until things get very bad indeed. Nurture openness and deep listening with your children.

- Be aware of children's play that suggests sexual knowledge beyond their years. Remember the peak year of vulnerability for a male child is age four. Children that young may not verbally describe an abusive episode—especially if they've been cautioned by the perpetrator not to do so. If you see behavior that may indicate something inappropriate has occurred, asking an inviting question such as, "Tell me how you know about that," may get the conversation going (even if the child's first answer is evasive, which may be another clue).

- Teach children and adolescents to disclose instances they believe are sexual abuse. Use the lists of acts at the beginning of this section to form judicious questions to better understand what your child reports. Unlike the past when children were more easily victimized because they didn't know they were permitted to refuse the sexual advances of an older child or adult, lots of kids now learn to *say no, get away,* and *tell someone.* Nonetheless you may not hear about abusive episodes because a young child fails to recognize the behavior as wrong or abusive. It may not *feel* right, but a child will tend to comply if he knows the perpetrator through family relationships, civic activities, or church involvements. When the child trusts the perpetrator, he'll tend to assume the activity is normal even though he hasn't encountered it elsewhere.

- Adolescents may conceal sexual abuse for precisely the opposite reason: They recognize the behavior is wrong and for reasons that make sense at the time—including bribery and threats—they respond with guilty compliance instead of justifiably angry defiance.

- In cases of incest, offending adults have been known to warn children that a parent may die if she discovers what they've been doing. Threats of physical harm to other family members or the victim are enough to keep kids in psychological bondage indefinitely. Special favors and the promise of gifts or privileges may be leveraged in an attempt to keep children quiet, though such tactics become less effective as children mature.

- It's possible that a naïve adolescent may not know that what was done to him was sexual abuse. Age-appropriate learning about physiology and sexuality are important to the whole-person growth of children, including their recovery should the worst happen.

- Post-traumatic stress must be included among the reasons adolescents might not disclose sexual abuse, especially sexualized violent assault—and all the more if it comes at the hands of someone they know. In 2003, seven of 10 female victims of rape or sexual assault identified a significant other, a relative, a friend, or an acquaintance as the attacker.[8] The stereotypical *unknown assailant* accounts for no more than a quarter of all rapes, but the stereotype leads to underreporting sexual abuse and assault. Just because the guy was a boyfriend doesn't alter the legal fact that forced penetration is rape. Just because it was Uncle Bud doesn't change the fact that forced fondling is sexual abuse. Too many young women and men accept behavior that should be reported as a crime, and they may even accept responsibility for what happened. A girl who believes she was raped because she *led her boyfriend* on and then *he couldn't stop* may not be willing to risk further retribution by telling her parents.

• It's possible you'll only learn about a sexual assault because the physical trauma of the attack requires medical attention—thus giving a child who might not otherwise risk disclosure no recourse because medical clinics and emergency units require parental consent before they'll treat a minor child. In that event focus on your child's well-being rather than your dismay.

JH: I don't know whether I heard this somewhere or just recognized the pattern; I only know there was a shift in the depth and breadth of my work with adolescents when I figured out that almost any significant crisis I mentioned in a serious manner was followed—usually pretty quickly—by a student who wanted to talk with me about that. I never knew a kid struggling with an eating disorder until I mentioned in a youth group talk that a lot of people struggle with eating disorders. After that I never ran out of people who wanted help with an eating disorder. The same is true of sexual abuse in all its forms, sexual identity issues, violence, substance addictions, and sexual compulsions. Adolescents are looking for open doors. I would rather your kid walk through your door than some others I can think of.

SIGNS OF SEXUAL ABUSE

It is somewhat easier to identify signs of abuse in small children than in teenagers.

- Be aware of children whose language and behavior indicate awareness and experience in sexuality that exceeds the unsophisticated curiosity displayed when little kids play *doctor*.

- Kids who have suffered recent sexual abuse may show physical signs such as soiled underwear or pain when sitting or walking.

- Abused children may be excessively physical in displays of emotion.

- Abused children may be inappropriately physical in displays of affection.

- Abused kids may be notably fearful of what they interpret as advances toward their bodies (a hand on the shoulder, for example).

- Emotional and physical withdrawal from relationships is common among sexually abused minors.

Adolescent victims usually want someone to intervene on their behalf, but they find the risk of disclosure very difficult to take. Things to watch for in combination:

- Numbing out

- Post-traumatic stress symptoms including flashbacks, nightmares and terrors, unprecedented zoning out, disengagement, and emotional hypersensitivity

- Self-injurious behaviors (SIB) including cutting, burning, or scratching

- Unprecedented sexual promiscuity

- Undue and inappropriately sustained affection and clinging to adults

- Unexpectedly deep depression

- Unprecedented nervousness, anxiety, or edginess

- Eating disorders. An unusually high percentage of women suffering eating disorders (80+ percent by some counts) are the victims of sexual abuse or assault

4.16 SEXUAL IDENTITY **CONFUSION**

How a young person defines his sexual identity affects everything—his feelings and opinions about himself and others; what he will and won't do with his body (or with another person's body); how he takes care of himself; his sense of what it means to be created in the image of God; where he thinks he fits in the world—his dreams, aspirations, and expectations—everything.

So how do girls come to think of themselves as girls? And how do boys become comfortable as boys—however comfortable that may be? Where does sexual identity come from? It's a big question.

NATURE VERSUS NURTURE

In a long-running debate, some people believe sexual identity is all about *nature*—plumbing and wiring determines sexual identity. The other side believes it's all about *nurture*—boys and girls *learn* to be boys and girls in their families and communities through a powerful process that overrides the effects of biochemistry.

These days there aren't many purists in the nature versus nurture debate. Most people acknowledge that having the plumbing and wiring in place doesn't mean people know how to behave. Biologically complete males and females learn the fine points of behaving like boys or girls from role models and trainers. Families, communities, and cultures *nurture* the *nature* of male and female children into the *behavior* of boys and girls. Over time, that socialization blossoms (or calcifies) into the adult patterns of women and men. And the research continues on the fundamentals of sexual identity.

Our Big Picture

Whatever scientists may learn in the future about our genetic nature, we already know a great deal about the effect childhood and pubescent experiences have on sexual identity. From those experiences we form a complex image of ourselves—how we perceive and make meaning, where we consciously or unconsciously place events in a bigger picture, and how we behave as a result.

When a boy is called a *sissy* or *faggot* because he doesn't throw a ball well or doesn't care about throwing a ball at all, that experience becomes part of his big picture. When a girl is called a *tomboy* or *butch* because she possesses unusual upper body strength or doesn't like dressing up, the teasing becomes part of her big picture. When a child of either gender is touched inappropriately by an older person of either gender, that touch shows up somewhere in the big picture. When children or adolescents are repeatedly asked by peers if they're gay or lesbian—or told they are—those questions and declarations are introduced to the big picture.

And what do individuals do with that big picture? That's the puzzle. Why one person becomes promiscuous and another is sexually repressed and a third seems to function along entirely conventional lines is as difficult to explain as it is to predict. Why one person comes to be more attracted to the male form and another to the female form is an equally complicated mystery. Who knows where to begin unraveling the ball of twine that creates sexual attraction?

The Story Behind the Story

We know this: Behind every story there's a story. Most of the time (not all the time but *most* of the time), once we hear the story behind the story, what people do (or did) begins to make a certain amount of sense. Not that the story behind the story excuses illegal or immoral acts, but it helps us interpret them.

So what does all this have to do with anything? For most of us, nothing. If we accept the most enthusiastic estimate of the number of homosexuals and bisexuals, we know that 90 percent of us will never make a single personal choice regarding homosexuality or bisexuality. Realistically though, many of us will have sexualized experiences that are confusing, perhaps even troubling, that have nothing to do with *being* homosexual or *being* bisexual.

We also know there's no excuse for bad behavior. The guy who seduces girls is not one iota better than the one who seduces other guys. And that has something to do with all of us because quite apart from the conversation about sexual identity, no one has the right to seduce another person.

Give Me a Sign

Sexual identity crises are self-defined. Apart from the most extreme behavioral affectations, there really aren't any signs of sexual identity confusion. Delicate men and rugged women fit within the range of normal for their genders. Having a great sense of style or loving softball are ridiculous measures of sexual identity. You can probably fill a page with masculine and feminine stereotypes that are equally shallow. Family and friends—and *especially* strangers—don't get to impose their will on an adolescent in a sexual identity crisis.

ACTION PLAN: BE FORTHRIGHT

- Don't joke about a child's sexual identity in public or private.

- Don't listen to jokes about a child's sexual identity in public or private.

- Don't put up with jokes about a child's sexual identity in your family.

- If necessary, get help to resolve your own sexual identity and behavioral choices.

- Take it *very* seriously if your child wants to talk with you about sexual identity issues. Not to do so may leave your child to face a threatening mix of risk factors all alone.

Self-identified bisexual and homosexual adolescents; those who have same-sex erotic encounters or report same-sex romantic attraction or relationships are at greater risk of—

- Assault—45 percent of homosexual men and 20 percent of homosexual women report being verbally or physically assaulted in high school specifically because of their sexual orientation; they're twice to four times as likely to be threatened with a weapon at school.

- Dropping out of school, being kicked out of home, and living on the street.

- Frequent and heavy use of tobacco, alcohol, marijuana, cocaine, and other drugs at an earlier age.

- Sexual intercourse, multiple partners, and rape.

- Sexually transmitted diseases, including HIV. (Homosexual girls have the lowest risk of STD infection; but lesbian adolescents are also likely to have had sexual intercourse with males, in which case the risk remains.)

- Suicide—they're anywhere from twice to seven times as likely to attempt suicide as self-identified heterosexual classmates.

- Psychosocial problems—stress, violence, lack of support, family problems, peer suicides, and homelessness.[1]

- If you're in a worshiping community, encourage youth leaders to teach a whole-person approach to sexuality. (Shameless plug: Ask spiritual leaders to evaluate *Good Sex: A Whole-Person Approach to Teenage Sexuality and God* by Jim Hancock and Kara Powell as a youth group resource.)

- Further shameless plug: Get copies of the student journal *What (Almost) Nobody Will Tell You about Sex* by Jim Hancock and Kara Powell for your teenager and for yourself, and then talk about what you read.

- Make it clear that you're open to talking about any issue of sexual behavior or sexual identity in a respectful, honest, and open way.

- If you have biblical convictions about sexual identity, don't quote the Bible selectively to make a point or to back your child into a corner.

- Don't draw distinctions between heterosexual, homosexual, and bisexual lust. Lust is lust. The implication that my lust is somehow better than my neighbor's lust is just ridiculous.

- Draw clear distinctions between sexual experiences and sexual identity. Many children experience various levels of same-gender preadolescent sex play with other children. Later, most see such experiences as child's play. A few attach more significance to those experiences in retrospect and need the assurance that it's a fairly common experience growing up. The presence of a much older child, adolescent, or adult in the story redefines an experience of child's play into a sexually abusive encounter. Some victims of childhood or early adolescent sexual abuse get the impression they may be homosexual or bisexual because of their sexualized encounters. Draw the distinction between child sex abuse and mature sexual identity. Some adolescents who say they're attracted to people of the same gender grow up to define themselves as heterosexual.

- Know this: You don't get to vote on your child's sexual attitudes, beliefs, and behaviors any more than she gets to vote on yours. You can listen, learn, advise, teach, guide, influence, monitor, seek to understand, and persuade; but in the end, you can't control how your child perceives her sexual identity. Nobody can. Apart from killing the child outright, your influence over her sexual identity and behavior is limited by your humanity. So if you can help it, don't slam doors. As long as you're still talking, there's hope for a positive outcome.

4.17 SEXUALLY TRANSMITTED **DISEASES**

Here's a snapshot of adolescent sexually transmitted infection data:

- Each year, about 3 million adolescents acquire a sexually transmitted disease—that's about one in four who are sexually active.

- A single act of unprotected sex exposes adolescent girls to a one percent risk of acquiring HIV, a 30 percent risk of contracting genital herpes, and a 50 percent chance of falling victim to gonorrhea.

- Chlamydia is more common among adolescent boys and girls than it is among adult men and women—in some test settings, as many as 29 percent of girls and 10 percent of boys tested positive for chlamydia.

- Adolescents have higher rates of gonorrhea than sexually active 20 to 44 year olds.

- Some studies of sexually active girls found infection rates up to 15 percent for human papillomavirus (HPV), which is linked to cervical cancer.

- The hospitalization rate for acute pelvic inflammatory disease (PID) is higher among adolescent girls than women. PID, most often the result of untreated chlamydia or gonorrhea, can lead to infertility and abnormal pregnancy.[1]

ACTION PLAN: SAY THE HARD THING (GENTLY)

- STDs are a medical problem with profound familial, social, and spiritual connections. Good *triage* demands treating the medical condition at the earliest possible date.

- Teach your children they can contract an infection from a single sexual contact.

- Teach your teenager to report suspected STDs to a physician. The impact of failing to treat HPV, gonorrhea, chlamydia, PID, and HIV range between awful and fatal. And that's not counting the likely spread of infection to others.

- Be aware that a significant number of adolescents are sexually active only briefly. This does not reduce the risk of that sexual contact, but it limits risk to that time frame. If you learn that your child has been sexually active, take him or her to a physician for testing.

- If you believe your child remains sexually active—even with one partner—insist on regular screening.

- Teach your sons and daughters to bring their friends to you for advice if they suspect an STD.

- In the event of a sexually transmitted infection, display compassion to the degree that you would want if you made the same mistake.

4.18 SUBSTANCE ABUSE **+ADDICTION**

At this writing, substance abuse among ninth through twelfth graders looks something like this:[1]

- Alcohol—74.3 percent drank alcohol at least once, 43.3 percent had at least one drink on at least one day during the previous month, and 25.5 percent had five or more drinks in succession on one or more days the previous month. Early drinking is increasing dramatically, with 19.3 percent of twelfth graders, 20.5 percent of eleventh graders, 26.5 percent of tenth graders, and 33.9 percent of ninth graders reporting they first drank before age 13.

- Cocaine—7.6 percent used cocaine at least once; 3.4 percent used cocaine one or more times during the previous month.

- Ecstasy—6.3 percent used ecstasy/MDMA at least once.

- Hallucinogens—8.5 percent used hallucinogenic drugs (LSD, PCP, Mescaline, etc.) at least once.

- Heroin—2.4 percent used heroin at least once.

- Inhalants—12.4 percent sniffed glue or inhaled the contents of aerosol sprays and paints to get high at least once.

- Injectable Drugs— 2.1 percent used a needle to inject any illegal drug at least once.

- Methamphetamines—6.2 percent used methamphetamines (speed, crystal, etc.) at least once.

- Marijuana—38.4 percent used marijuana at least once; 20.2 percent used marijuana one or more times the previous month. Early marijuana use is increasing, with 6.2 percent of twelfth graders, 7.1 percent of eleventh graders, 9.1 percent of tenth graders, and 11.2 percent of ninth graders reporting they first tried marijuana before age 13.

- Nicotine—54.3 percent tried smoking at least once; 23 percent smoked in the previous month; 10.7 percent of those smoked 10 or more cigarettes each day they smoked; 54.6 percent of them tried to quit smoking the previous year; 8 percent used smokeless tobacco the previous month; 14 percent smoked cigars the previous month.

- Steroids—4 percent took steroid pills or shots without a doctor's prescription at least once.

Alcohol and nicotine are unchallenged for lethality and public health costs. The baseline for direct alcohol-attributable deaths in the United States is nearly 76,000 each year, at a cost of 2.3 million years of potential life lost.[2] The economic impact is estimated at more than $26 billion in direct medical and mental health costs, $134 billion in lost productivity, and $24 billion in motor vehicle crashes, crime, fire destruction, and social welfare costs. That's a grand total of about $185 billion annually.[3]

Every year about 440,000 Americans die of cigarette-attributable causes, costing 5.6 million years of potential life lost and $75 billion in direct medical costs, plus $82 billion in lost productivity— about $157 billion annually.[4]

WHY?

Unless we understand *why* teenagers use alcohol and other drugs, that data is interesting but useless.

Curiosity

Adolescents are all about the new experience: 81.7 percent of high school students report having one or more drinks at least once by twelfth grade (trending sharply upward at this writing).

Imitation

In *Nobody Knows My Name* James Baldwin writes: "The situation of our youth is not mysterious. Children have never been very good at listening to their elders but they have never failed to imitate them. They must, they have no other models."[5]

Baldwin was writing about something else at the time, but he put his finger right on a larger truth: We are raising children in a drugged culture—an adult beverage in one hand and prescription pills in the other—trying to make ourselves understood around the hand-rolled cigar between our teeth. *I need a drink...Don't talk to me, I haven't had my coffee yet...*it doesn't take kids long to learn the distinction between enjoying a glass of wine at dinner and needing a little something to take the edge off. Many parents encourage self-medication because example has always taught more than instruction.

To make matters more difficult, refusal skills come hard to adolescents whose friends are their lifeblood. Come Friday night it takes a lot of ego strength to face ridicule or rejection for standing against the popular will.

The psychologist and professor David Elkind speaks of teenagers who develop a "patchwork self"—an identity constructed by the simple addition of feelings, thoughts, and beliefs copied from others. Teenagers "who have grown by substitution and only have a patchwork self are less able to postpone immediate gratification.

They are present-oriented and other-directed, easily influenced by others."[6] That's not every kid all the time, but it's a big number much of the time.

Fun

It's possible that nothing holds greater sway than self-defined fun. You know the gag:

"Did you have fun last night?

"Oh man, I was so tweaked. I don't remember where I was or what I did. I woke up in a pool of my own urine—at least I think it was mine."

"Dude!"

"I have a chipped tooth."

"Dude!"

"I found the beginning of a tattoo on my ankle. I think it was gonna be My Little Pony."

"No way!"

"I don't know how I got home or what happened to my car— or my underwear."

"Dude!"

"I never had so much fun in my life."

"Sweet!"

You have to admit it's difficult to have that kind of fun sober. And as long as that urine thing doesn't become chronic and My Little Pony doesn't get infected and the car doesn't show up in a crime report and a 30-year-old dude doesn't show up in a Trans Am...with the underwear, then it will remain a cherished *memory*—well, not a memory exactly.

Declaration of Independence

One young man said he started smoking pot "because all my parents ever talk about is how bad drugs are!" Marijuana was a way of letting his parents know that he intended to do as he pleased.

The therapist Gary Forrest was among the first to describe the phenomenon:

> Studies indicate that over 80 percent of families in which both parents drink produce children who drink. To the contrary, over 70 percent of parents who do not drink produce children who abstain. However, there are cases where complete parental abstinence from alcohol actually encourages the teenager to drink. If drinking is taboo in the family, then the contrary-minded teenager may conclude that drinking must be fun. For some teenagers, drinking offers a great way to upset and control parents who are non-drinkers.[7]

Disinhibition

I drink because it helps me be myself. I'm more creative when I'm wired. Being a little toasty helps me get so much deeper into the music. Placebo studies in which college students were told a drink contained alcohol when it didn't found that those who *expected* to experience disinhibiting effects from the alcohol tended to get what they expected (some even reported feeling drunk)—in spite of the absence of alcohol in the drinks.[8]

Escape

Teenagers use alcohol and other drugs to escape the pain of fractured or abusive relationships, feelings of inadequacy, fear of the future, school pressure, parental expectations—almost any stressor can lead to self-medication. The biggest challenge to parents discouraging drug use is that drugs *work*. At least for a while. Many users affirm that temporary relief is better than none at all.

Addiction

Regular use of some substances creates chemical dependency. The heavy caffeine user who goes off his beverage of choice for any reason (say Lent or a backpacking trip) knows something about withdrawal symptoms such as headaches, irritability, and disrupted sleep patterns—and that's just caffeine.

Trying to juggle the physical and psychological impact of a drug with progressive tolerance that demands more frequent use but delivers less of the desired effect gradually turns into a full-time job for addicts. When he was director of the National Institute on Drug Abuse, Alan Leshner wrote the essence of addiction is "uncontrollable, compulsive drug seeking and use, even in the face of negative health and social consequences."[9] *Compulsive seeking and use no matter what*...that about covers it.

TOLERANCE

Tolerance is the key difference between an alcoholic and a problem drinker. There is evidence that everyone has the potential for problem drinking. Problem drinkers have problems when they drink and lots of problems when they drink lots. On the other hand, one telltale sign of a budding alcoholic is his capacity to absorb large quantities of alcohol without obvious impairment—it's often the alcoholic who drives the problem drinker home from a party.

This is not good news. Tolerance to high blood alcohol levels is an early sign that poisonous levels of alcohol will eventually be required to produce an intoxicating effect. Later still it will take poisonous levels to just feel normal. No one can poison herself on a regular basis without sustaining long-term organic damage. Better to be a lightweight when it comes to alcohol tolerance; better to face the music if you're not.

ACTION PLAN: ENGAGE

Don't immediately jump to conclusions when certain factors seem to indicate involvement with drugs. By the same token don't deny what's right in front of you. The presence of one or two of the factors commonly associated with substance abuse may only indicate that a teenager is experiencing changes typical of adolescence; but even when they suspect there's a problem most parents err *not* on the side of overreacting but in waiting too long to act. If the concerns are reality-based, it's better to be safe than sorry.

Signs of Teenage Alcohol and Drug Abuse

- Withdrawal—spending significantly more time alone in her room (or another secluded place) than before; uncharacteristic avoidance of interaction and fun with the family

- Inexplicable relational shifts—dumping valued friends and rapid bonding with a new circle of associates; being secretive about names, times, and places

- Difficulties in school—unprecedented truancy, uncompleted assignments, loss of concentration, unexpected decline in grades

- Unreasonable resistance to reasonable authority—unprecedented sustained conflict with parents, teachers, police, youth workers, or other adults

- Inexplicably shifting interests—loss of interest in personal hygiene, grooming, neatness, play, creativity, friendships

- Behavior problems—stealing, shoplifting, lying, or unexplained spending

- High-risk behaviors—loss of regard for personal safety, frequent traffic violations, vandalism

- Persistent signs of depression—suicidal talk or gesturing, actual suicide attempt

- Sexual promiscuity—indiscreet sexual behavior, multiple partners

- Health complaints—unprecedented frequent colds, flu, vomiting, constipation, abdominal distress, headaches, tremors

- Changes in eating habits—unaccountable increase or decrease in appetite with accompanying weight gain or loss

- Obvious signs of being under the influence—alcohol on the breath, slurred speech, staggering, dilated pupils, exhilaration, hallucinations, panic, delusions, heart palpitations, unprecedented unselfconscious body odor, sleeplessness

Remember the qualifiers in these descriptions—*inexplicable, unprecedented, persistent.* You don't want to leap to conclusions, but you also don't want to ignore clusters of suspicious behavior.

If you doubt your perceptions, here are some questions to help you assess what you've experienced.

- When did you first believe there might be a problem?

- How did you respond to that realization?

- What is the substance of the conversations you've had with your child about this?

- What has your child admitted? Would a reasonable adult see that as cause for concern?

- What has your child explained away? Would a reasonable adult buy these explanations?

- What natural consequences has your child experienced because of her behavior? (Lost and damaged property and hangovers are *natural consequences.*) How did she handle that?

- What logical consequences have you enforced? (Restriction from driving and strict curfews are *logical consequences.*) How did she respond?

- What indicators do you have that the problem is better or worse than it was 30 days ago?

- What does your gut tell you?

- What makes you trust or distrust your instincts about this?

- What would you like to see happen?

- Do you believe you have the resources to get there?

- What obstacles stand in the way?

- What kind of help do you believe you could use?

- Who would be able to lend that help?

If there appears to be cause for concern but it still feels intangible to you, ask the kid you're concerned about to keep you company on a daylong road trip.

- Take him out of school for the day, leaving early enough so he can't sleep in.

- Drive for three or four hours with limited stops until you get to whatever destination you've chosen for whatever business you've elected to conduct. (It doesn't really matter what that business is, but it would be nice if it were something about which he might contribute an opinion.)

- A couple times along the way, thank him for accompanying you on what probably seems to him like a fairly pointless mission. Tell him it's nice to have his company.

- Ask open-ended questions that require stories rather than conceptual answers. Start with subjects that are personal but non-threatening, and move gradually and naturally toward questions that invite greater disclosure—music preferences, sports, favorite television shows, and movies. He'll be wary, but you can almost certainly outlast him, especially as you reciprocate with stories of your own.

- Note his physical posture and endurance, his apparent emotional state and vocabulary, his degree of tolerance for and engagement in conversation, and his ability to remain focused on a conversational thread.

- When you reach your destination, make sure you leave the vehicle and walk around a bit, including stairs or a hill. Eat something. Make small talk comparing your destination with where you live.

- On the return trip, ask open-ended questions that call for stories about his imagined future, as well as his remembered past.

- Thank him again for the company as you say goodnight.

- The next morning, reflect privately on his behavior and apparent attitudes the night before and his getting up and out of the home in the morning.

This approach will cost you a day, but you'll almost certainly have a better notion of whether there's an emerging threat and whether further intervention is appropriate. In the process there's a fair chance your teenager will reveal—or you'll otherwise discover—something about the story behind the story.

By the way, if the issue turns out to be alcohol, don't underestimate the hazard: *Oh, it's only alcohol—I was afraid he was doing drugs!* In general, the consequences of alcohol abuse are far more lethal than other drugs. Don't rob a young alcoholic or problem drinker of the opportunity for early intervention because you don't want to see what you're seeing.

Review chapter 3.0 in this book for the processes involved in calling in reinforcements and developing an action plan.

Most communities now have effective outpatient and in-hospital programs to help adolescents grapple with alcohol and drug dependencies. Most programs require family involvement in the treatment because a user's potential for long-term recovery is much greater when family members embrace the important role they play in the process.

4.19 SUICIDE

Someone now forgotten spoke of suicide in the context of a *biological, sociocultural, interpersonal, dyadic, existential malaise*—which is a verbal way of shielding the truth that no one is really sure why people take their own lives. Suicide is a stew without a recipe cooked up over weeks, months, even years.

Adolescents, who are by nature more impulsive than adults, sometimes pose a lethal exception to this description. An especially painful breakup may be enough to drive a 15-year-old boy to kill himself out of the blue. But not usually. Most of the time the straw that breaks the camel's back is no more the "cause" of the suicide than any other single factor.

Most suicides can be prevented. In fact, we think most suicides *are* prevented—in the sense that they never materialize. The majority of suicidal kids walk the balance beam between "I really, really want to die" and "I really, really want to live." If there's a single word that describes the suicidal disposition, it's *ambivalence*.

There's a great story about a rookie cop on his first suicide call. He makes his way onto the roof of a 30-story office building and finds a man teetering on the ledge. Instinctively, the young officer pulls his service revolver and shrieks, "Freeze!" At which the guy on the ledge throws his hands in the air and yells, "Don't shoot!" as if to say *If you shoot me, I might die!*—a strange sentiment for someone who moments earlier contemplated becoming one with the pavement below. That's ambivalence.

GIVE ME A SIGN

Here are some risk factors that may foreshadow a suicidal act:

- A history of developmental problems

- Escalating family problems

- Acute experience of separation and loss

- Feelings of rejection and being unwanted

- Chronic communication problems

- Obvious and abrupt behavioral changes

- Sustained extreme moodiness and withdrawal

- Repeated involvement in high-risk behaviors

- Abuse of alcohol and other drugs

- Medically undiagnosed physical complaints

- Perfectionism

- Despair

- Giving away treasured objects

- Suicidal notes

- Suicidal language: *I'd be better off dead. You won't have to worry about me much longer. No one cares if I'm around. I'll just end it all.*

- A common thread in many suicides is a history of problems piling up one after another with no end in sight. When helplessness combines with hopelessness, adolescents are at serious risk.

- Sudden, unexplained emotional release from a chronic depression. Counselors working with chronically depressed people warn that a sudden, drastic elevation in mood may mask a suicidal intention. Depressed people sometimes muster just enough energy to conclude that suicide is the only way to end their pain. Once ultimate resolution is in sight, they may experience an extravagant emotional release.

ACTION PLAN: INVESTIGATE FURTHER

- Take suicide language and gestures seriously—even if your kid brushes you off with claims that he would never do anything that stupid. Pay attention to repeated mentions of death, especially in the presence of a cluster of risk factors.

- Look and listen for unverbalized emotion. Suicidal teenagers often have difficulty articulating the pain they feel and the hopelessness and helplessness of their situations. Worse, they may believe their cries for help have gone unheeded. For some, suicidal gestures are efforts to gain attention and get help. Suicide has been referred to as a *perverse language*; as if the suicidal person were saying, "If you won't hear me, I'll make you listen—because you can't ignore a dead body!"

- If you have the faintest reason to believe your child's use of suicidal language may be serious, engage him in a private conversation to investigate. Use the SLAP outline in section 2.2 to guide your questioning.

  - **S**pecific Plans: Does he have a plan?

  - **L**ethal Method: Is his method deadly?

  - **A**vailability of Method: Does he have access to his intended means?

  - **P**roximity of Helping Resources: Will his plan put him out of reach?

- If you believe the risk is immediate, seek medical intervention right away. Put the child in the car or call a cab and drive him to a doctor's office or emergency room. If you feel you need to restrain him, get one or more adults to accompany you and make him sit between them. If necessary, call 911 for an ambulance or law enforcement. They'll ask you if your child is a danger to himself or to others. Tell them yes in no uncertain terms. Even if your child has not harmed himself, medical personnel will know what to do.

- Ask the question: "Have you considered suicide?" There are two typical responses—*No, things aren't that bad*, or *Yes, I have.* If the answer is *no*, then you've opened a door for preventive care. *I'm glad to know that it hasn't gotten that bad; will you promise me that if it does, you'll talk with me before you take any action?* If the answer is *yes*, then you've really asked the right question.

- Believe you can help. Don't ignore obvious warnings like, *I'll just kill myself, and then they'll be happy!* You can be a bridge to life for your child in a suicidal crisis; a degree in counseling or specialized training is not required to make a difference. Do your part and ask for help from others who can do what you can't.

Contract for Life

Engage your child in a *Contract for Life.* Suicide prevention programs across the country utilize such written agreements because they have proven useful in saving lives. The agreement can be made verbally, but evidence suggests that a written document is more effective. A typical contract looks like this:

Contract for Life

I _____ promise not to harm myself or attempt to kill myself.
  TEENAGER

If I feel like killing myself, I will talk with _____,
                                                   MOM AND/OR DAD

and if I am unable to reach him/her, I will call _____
                                                     OTHER TRUSTED ADULT

or the Crisis Hotline at 1-800-SUICIDE and speak honestly with a crisis worker.
If all else fails, I will dial 911.

_____   _____
  TEENAGER   DATE

_____   _____
  PARENT(S)   DATE

It's worth noting that kids have been known to take the terms of the contract more legalistically than one would hope. Make sure your contract says *talk with* not *try to talk with*. Sometimes a young person who has attempted suicide after agreeing to a contract has defended herself saying, "You asked me to *try* to contact you first. I *did* and you weren't available!" So if you use a contract, do everything in your power to make yourself available on a 24-hour basis because a teenager in crisis may not be able to limit the struggle to your waking hours. Your willingness to drop everything presents a believable message of compassion.

- Deal with the method. Clear your house of guns for the duration of the crisis; take the car keys; lock away your medications and kitchen knives. If your child claims to possess the means, tell him you want to hold onto or dispose of it until the crisis is passed. Doing so reduces the possibility of an impulsive act. That said, don't use physical force to take control of a lethal object or you may find yourself with a different crisis on your hands.

- Be willing to involve the police if necessary.

- Develop an action plan. (See section 3.2.)

Here's good news: The average suicidal episode is only 30 days in duration and only one in 10 who seriously attempts to take his life will try again. This means suicide intervention is unlikely to become a lifestyle for you. If you get a teenager through a serious episode, you've probably saved his life.

If the worst happens, do what you can to take care of the survivors. "Murder is a crime of violence against the murdered person," one of Salman Rushdie's characters says and, "Suicide is a crime of violence against those who remain alive."[1] Being the ones who remain alive in the aftermath of suicide isn't easy. Those who live on will experience many of the same emotions as those who lose a family member or friend by accidental or natural death: Shock, anger, guilt, fear, and relief are common to all sorts of losses. But these emotions may be experienced in different ways and to different degrees after a suicide.

- *Secure your own mask first.* Make sure you get the help you need even as you begin looking after the well-being of your family.

- Those left behind must deal with *shock and disbelief* not only because of the loss, but also because the death was self-inflicted. Questions such as *Can I go on without this person?* are compounded by questions such as *What in the world just happened here?*

- Anger is frequently directed at the deceased for being so self-absorbed. Those left behind may blame themselves for not being sensitive enough, for ignoring warnings, or for not saying or doing whatever would've made the difference. Even God is a likely target. *If God is so wise and powerful, why allow this to happen?*

- Death brings out the *guilt* in people. We wonder if we should have done this or that and whether it might have changed things. Little children are notorious for wondering if they should have behaved better and if that would have prevented mommy or daddy from feeling bad enough to want to die.

- Those still living wonder if they can go on investing in relationships and may *fear* initiating new ones. They seriously question the saying: "Better to have loved and lost than never to have loved at all." The vulnerability required by a relationship may seem like more than they can handle.

- Few emotions create more conflicts in the hearts and minds of the living than the sense of *relief* that sometimes follows the suicide of someone with a history of difficulties that became a heavy burden for family and friends. The loss is tragic, but there can also be a sense of relief that it's finally over—which may lead to guilty feelings and self-loathing.

- The *shame* associated with suicide is difficult for surviving family and friends to work through. It's not easy acknowledging that a loved one's death was a suicide. Some have trouble even saying the word.

- It's not unusual for physical and emotional difficulties to surface in the wake of suicide, among them: headaches, bouts of uncontrollable crying, fatigue, sleeplessness—in short, all the physical and emotional baggage that travels with any crisis. Someone (we forget who) observed, "We all have skeletons in our closet. A suicide is someone who leaves his or her skeleton in someone else's closet." That's not a bad characterization. Some things change very slowly. Many of us have deep-seated emotional problems because we've been unwilling or unable to confront the skeletons in our closets. The challenge in helping survivors cope lies in their willingness to identify the continuing influence of their skeletons, admit their fear of getting too close, and work to get rid of the blasted things.

RVP: I was invited to do a suicide prevention workshop at a military installation that had experienced a rash of suicide attempts and completions by dependent kids of military personnel. The post chaplain arranged for me to have dinner with a mom and dad whose son had committed suicide a year prior to my visit. No mention of the boy or circumstances of his death were discussed during dinner.

When we moved to the family room for coffee and dessert, I approached the subject by asking if I might see a picture of their son, acknowledging that I was aware of his fairly recent death. His mom began crying uncontrollably. When she regained composure, I apologized for any insensitivity I might have displayed.

She quickly countered with, "Oh, no, please don't feel badly. It's just that in the year since our son's death, you're the first person who has asked about him." Well-meaning friends and family avoided the subject because they were afraid they might cause further pain, unaware that their avoidance caused more pain than they ever imagined.

The point is to get rid of the skeleton—not the memory of the loved one.

- Well-meaning friends and family often avoid talking about the circumstances of the suicide or initiating discussion about the deceased altogether. That's not helpful—survivors crave the openness of people who will take time to listen as they share wide-ranging emotions. That's how people embrace the hope that life will go on for them.

- That said, some survivors need the skills of a trained therapist to help them deal with their skeletons. Do what you can to facilitate that as necessary. You may benefit greatly from family or couples counseling where you can work through issues of grief together. Suicide creates profound stress on marriages. Some people find help in specialized post-suicide or child-loss support groups.

- Correct people's misconceptions about suicide:

  - *Anyone who tries to kill himself has got to be crazy.* Not crazy; hopeless. Hopelessness produces a loss of perspective that can make suicide seem like a viable option because the person has lost the ability to see other options. Perfectionism produces a chronic dread of failure that makes the future appear threatening rather than promising. Relational isolation feeds the perception of aloneness and clouds the memory of good times in the past. Hopelessness is associated with poor judgment, especially when mixed with alcohol or other depressants. In the absence of hope—distorted though that perspective may be—a significant setback or loss can have deadly consequences.

  - *Rich kids kill themselves more often because they're bored with life.* Suicide is a truly democratic phenomenon. Rich kids kill themselves; poor kids kill themselves. White kids, Black kids, Irish kids, Norwegian kids—all God's children have the capacity to kill themselves. But mainly it's adults who kill themselves. The suicide rate for 10-to-14-year-olds is less than two in 100,000; for 15-to-19-year-olds the rate hovers near eight suicide deaths for every 100,000; and 20-to-34-year-olds kill themselves at a rate of nearly 13 for every 100,000. The rates continue to rise in the next two age groups—which is important to note because many of the people within these cohorts are the parents of adolescents—about 15 out of every 100,000 among 35-to-44-year-olds and 16 out of every 100,000 among 45-to-54-year-olds.[2]

  - *Suicide runs in her family.* No genetic markers have been found to indicate an inherited predisposition toward suicide. That said, there are *suicidogenic* family patterns that increase the likelihood of suicide. If a parent, older sibling, or someone extremely close commits suicide when kids are young, those children may grow up viewing suicide as an acceptable way of coping—after all, that's what Grandpa did. Suicide acquires the standing of *learned behavior* for them. Later they may be more inclined than their peers to view suicide as a coping tactic. There may be *suicidogenic* conditions in some communities and schools where cluster suicides give the impression of normalcy. So ask yourself: *Has my child seen suicide modeled as a way out?*

- *She killed herself on that gloomy Wednesday. The weather must have depressed her.* You'd think. But a higher percentage of suicides take place in nice weather—more in spring than winter, for example. When the weather is gloomy, many people are depressed, and misery loves company. But when nice weather comes along and most people's spirits are elevated, the misery of depressed people is intensified.

- *Better stay with her tonight! That's when most suicides happen.* Actually, most adolescent suicides occur when kids are home alone—between three and six in the afternoon.

- *There was something romantic about their suicides. They loved each other so much—they wanted to die together.* Anyone who has been at the scene of a suicide knows there's nothing romantic or beautiful about it.

- *She didn't leave a note. There were no clues. It couldn't have been a suicide.* At most, one in four people who commit suicide leaves a note. When suicides increased in North America, police departments and researchers started conducting *psychological autopsies* to reconstruct the patterns and interactions of suicidal people. Their findings demonstrate conclusively that the majority of suicide victims provided

✦

verbal or behavioral clues. Unfortunately, those clues were often missed until it's too late.

- *Suicide is the unpardonable sin! She'll never be forgiven.* There's nothing in the Bible that represents suicide as a sin that God is either unwilling or unable to forgive. We certainly don't welcome the news of any suicide, but we affirm the goodness of God who, even when we are faithless, remains faithful.[3]

- Teach perspectives and skills that enliven resilience in adolescents. In no particular order, resilient kids learn:

  - Not to take hardship personally

  - Not to blame themselves for the choices of others

  - To adapt to change and to recover from disappointment

  - That every condition, pleasant or unpleasant, is temporary

  - To endure difficulty and pain

  - A rich emotional vocabulary

  - Negotiation skills

  - Empathy

  - Adaptability

  - To laugh at their own humanness

  - Appropriate risk taking in hope of appropriate reward

  - Flexibility

4.20 TERROR

Earthquakes...Terrorism...Fires...Hurricanes...Industrial Accidents...
Tornadoes...Mass Murders...

Apart from acquainting them with the God of mercy, there's not much you can do to prepare the young for an asteroid strike. It's just one of those things. To a slightly lesser degree, this is also true of hurricanes, tornadoes, earthquakes, blizzards, fires, and floods. Add catastrophic disease to the same list. And divorce, plane crashes, and train derailments. And serial killers, car bombers, and kidnappers.

These are the things that come out of nowhere to disrupt life-as-we-know-it. Even one of Job's *comforters*—pausing in the middle of hammering Job with his conviction that bad things happen mainly to bad people—had to admit that as surely as sparks fly upward, our sort are born to trouble.[1] Or as a Hemingway character says in *A Farewell to Arms*: "The world breaks everyone."[2]

Smart people argue about which is worse, natural or human-caused disasters—some research suggests trauma symptoms are more persistent in the aftermath of human-caused events—but that may be splitting hairs. When the dead are dead, the injured broken, the buildings tumbled, communications scrambled, dreams dashed, and hope dimmed, it doesn't make much immediate difference what caused it. Later maybe—but not until the terror subsides.

Terror is that overwhelming fear that all hell is breaking loose and there's nothing to be done about it. The most expansive terrors leave high body counts and lots of people injured, dislocated, and exposed to secondary health and safety dangers. These nightmare scenarios continue to reverberate, wrecking economies and social networks, leaving the survivors shocked, then skittish, then afraid and sad for a very long time.

Are these wide-ranging terrors worse than the intensely personal trauma of rape or murder? Who knows? The post-traumatic stress symptoms are similar. The big ones may simply be bigger, visited upon more victims.

Here's the gotcha: Regardless of its nature—no matter how public or private it may be—by the time terror hits, it's too late to prepare for it and too late to stop it—otherwise it wouldn't produce terror.

If we've learned anything, it's that we can't get away with bluffing kids—not for long. We can't really promise to keep them safe because once they realize it's beyond our capacity, they'll stop trusting us. If kids come to believe we are untrustworthy, that's just one more loss in a world that already feels pretty dangerous.

Here's a partial list of terrors parents can't promise to prevent:

- Weather-related disasters

- Earthquakes and tsunamis

- Asteroid strikes

- Communicable diseases

- Physical and sexual assaults

- Terrorist attacks and acts of war

- Criminality, school shootings, and random acts of violence

- Economic and financial ruin

- Accidents

- Genetic defects

- Our own death

Here's a fairly comprehensive list of what parents can promise:

1. I'll do my best to protect you every day.

2.

There is no number two. It's sad the list can't be more extensive, but this is reality—so there you have it.

ACTION PLAN: PREPARE AND RESPOND

Before terror strikes, here are some things you can do to prepare your children for the worst:

- Promise to do your best to protect them every day.

- Develop a disaster plan together. Make sure everyone knows how to:

  - Dial 911

  - Reach extended family and trusted friends by phone

  - Turn off the gas and reset the electrical breakers

  - Locate flashlights, batteries, portable AM/FM radio, candles, matches, fresh water, and nonperishable food

  - Locate home on a map

  - Walk to the nearest medical facility

  - Locate and preserve insurance policies, wills, and financial records

- Agree on where you'll meet if you're separated and can't get home following a disaster.

- Identify a secondary meeting place if you can't get to the first one

- Identify a third place to meet if you can't reach the others

- Agree on who will stay put at whichever meeting place they can reach and who will move from location one to location two to location three until everyone is reunited

- Develop a personal disaster agreement to address more private terrors

  - Communicate convincingly that no event can destroy your loving commitment—not pregnancy, HIV/AIDS, substance abuse, sexual assault, or murder.

  - Agree on a plan to disclose bad news, including getting help making the disclosure, if necessary, rather than sitting on it.

After terror hits there is much a parent can do.

- As the shock subsides, ask, "Now what?" Give kids a reason to think into the future about recovery, rebuilding, and prevention.

- Lead your family in serving others in age-appropriate (and situationally appropriate) ways. In general, think about starting near at hand and working outward, always looking for unmet needs you can responsibly address.

- Speak into the terror theologically.

  - One of the most potent messages in the face of catastrophe is the declaration, "It's not supposed to be like this." If we're anywhere near right about the God they talk about in the Bible, our Creator takes no pleasure in the suffering and death of his creatures.

The companion piece to the declaration, "It's not supposed to be like this," is the affirmation, "And someday it won't be." The hope of the gospel includes *a new heaven and a new earth—the home of righteousness*. We haven't seen it, but in faith we see it coming. In the meantime life is grace *and* bad things happen; people are capable of breathtaking displays of love *and* staggering acts of oppression; the sun rises and the rain falls on the righteous *and* the unrighteous. Life is hard; God is good.

- Watch for signs of post-traumatic stress disorder (see section 4.12).

PRE-FLIGHT INSTRUCTIONS

The nice people who look after our safety on airplanes give a little speech at the beginning of each flight, reminding us that in the unlikely event of cabin depressurization an oxygen mask will drop down from the overhead panel. We are to grasp the masks just so, put them over our noses and mouths, tighten the elastic straps, and breathe normally.

It seems safe to say we probably don't want to know what kind of force it takes to depressurize the cabin of a jetliner—enough to wreak quite a bit of havoc. So flight attendants end this part of their presentation with the admonition to secure our own masks before assisting children or others who may need help. This is good advice because if there's a disaster you're as likely to be terrorized as anyone else. So take a deep breath and pull yourself together as fast as you can. Then start looking around for someone who's turning blue.

4.21 TROUBLE WITH **THE LAW**

If your kid gets in trouble with the law for any but the most minor infractions:

- Don't go it alone. Involve trusted family members and friends sooner rather than later. You'll need their support and perspective.

- Don't be afraid to go into detention facilities. (It's the fear of the unknown—easily overcome, but not until it's acknowledged.) Unless your child is charged with a violent offense you're likely to find an open door from people in the legal system.

- Don't forget that a kid in trouble is still a kid. The biggest difference between most kids in trouble with the law and a whole lot of other kids is that some got caught while others didn't. That's a bit of an exaggeration, but honestly, kids are kids. Truly evil kids are rare and in a different class than most juvenile offenders. If you're dealing with an evil child, you probably didn't need an arresting officer to tell you so.

- Maintain perspective. Sometimes good parents have good kids who make bad decisions and get in trouble.

ACTION PLAN: ENGAGE THE SYSTEM

- Whether a teenager is apprehended for a relatively minor offense such as shoplifting or is charged with a more serious offense such as robbery, the legal procedures used by most jurisdictions follow the same pattern.

    - Generally when a suspected offender is arrested or brought in for questioning, an intake evaluation is completed. This includes gathering information from the arresting officer and the juvenile. If the offense is relatively minor and there are no prior offenses, a *lecture-release* may be deemed appropriate, in which case the young offender and his parent or guardian are given a warning and sent home. Otherwise a probable cause hearing is set to determine whether or not sufficient evidence exists to justify continuance of the complaint.

    - If probable cause is established, a trial date is set before a juvenile court judge or in certain situations a judge and jury.

    - The young person may be remanded to the custody of his parent or guardian or to a juvenile detention facility to await trial.

    - During the entire process, some offenders will be detained in a juvenile facility because of prior offenses, severity of the crime, inability to post bond, unwillingness of custodial parents to receive the minor child back into their custody because the child is beyond their control, high flight risk, or any other factor the court believes might prevent the juvenile from appearing for the next phase of the process.

    - If the juvenile judge or the judge and jury decide the evidence at trial proves guilt beyond reasonable doubt, then a disposition hearing is set. During the hearing the judge weighs recommendations from the prosecution and defense, considers the statutory options, and renders a verdict spelling out the treatment or punitive measures ordered by the court.

- Take time to understand the policies and procedures of the jurisdiction in which your child is held so you can better understand his day-to-day situation. Incarceration is terribly difficult for most adolescents no matter how self-assured they may appear on the surface.

- Push through your discomfort and work to develop genuine connections with line staff, counselors, and chaplains within the institution. You'll enjoy greater freedom if those in charge see you as cooperative, trustworthy, and not antagonistic.

- Learn to be a deep listener. Institutionalized kids learn quickly that anything they say *can and probably will be* used against them. Your child may even become suspicious of you for a time and tend to shy away from anything deeper than a surface connection. In *At Risk: Bringing Hope to Hurting Teenagers,* Dr. Scott Larson writes:

Erick Erikson has pointed out that unless the issue of trust is resolved for a young person, that person will remain stunted in emotional (and spiritual) development. Honesty, consistency, and a stable presence through both good and bad times are what lay the critical foundation of trust. Our role is not to fix teenagers but to be there for them. And this, over time, will lay a foundation for God to bring into their lives others with whom they can build relationships of trust as well.[1]

- There's not much to look forward to in lockup. If your child remains in custody, keep the promises you make and don't make promises you may not be able to keep. If you say you're going to visit on a particular day, be there or have a note from your doctor. If you can't be there, call to let him know you're sorry.

- Leave books, magazines, and CDs (if permissible). Kids living in institutions generally have too much free time and may welcome fresh reading and listening material.

- Be there when your child gets out. Re-entry is tough. Do what you can to help your child succeed at do-overs.

TREATMENT FACILITIES

After a brush with the law, some parents are inclined to place the offending teenager in a private residential treatment facility. Acknowledging the pain and heartbreak of coping with a wildly out-of-control child, we nevertheless encourage you to exhaust every other possible measure before relinquishing your adolescent's emotional health and well-being to people in an institutional setting. The behavior modification programs utilized in many of these facilities mainly teach kids how to play the game more effectively. Most of the young people we've seen placed in residential treatment facilities have only become more adept in their acting out behaviors as a result of being thrust into a community of like-minded peers.

4.22 VIOLENCE

American teenagers are about two and a half times more likely than adults to be victims of non-fatal violent crimes—about two-thirds of which are committed in residences between three and six in the afternoon. With the exception of simple assault—where no weapon is used and victims suffer no serious bodily harm—the juvenile crime arrest rate is at its lowest in a generation. That said, the arrest rate for simple assault is more than double what it was in 1980. Whether the rise in arrests reflects increased violence or just better reporting is unclear.

About one in eight high school students is involved in a physical conflict at school each year. In a given month, five percent of high school students respond to fear of school-related crime by staying home one or more days.[1]

That snapshot of non-lethal violence among American adolescents is by no means perfect, nor is it as grim as many people imagine. The picture of lethal violence among adolescents is more sobering, if only because it is, by definition, deadly. Based on joint findings by the U. S. Department of Education and the Secret Service, here is what we know about kids who aim to kill fellow students and school personnel.[2]

- Targeted school violence is rarely a sudden, impulsive act. Attackers at school go to extraordinary lengths in conceiving and planning violence. About half develop the idea of the attack for at least a month, and most prepare their attack for at least two days.

- Few attackers are loners or losers. Most appear to be mainstream kids. Most live in two-parent homes. Most are doing reasonably well in school. Few have been in serious trouble at school. Few have histories of violence toward others or cruelty to animals. Many are involved in organized social groups inside or outside school. Nearly all act alone, but a wide majority has close friends.

- Almost all attackers engage in behavior that signals a need for help. Most tell at least one peer that they're thinking about or planning an attack. In most cases at least one adult is concerned by pre-attack behavior. About 60 percent display an interest in violent movies, books, games, or personal writings—but there's no single common medium.

- More than half of attackers are motivated by revenge. Most feel bullied, threatened, attacked, or injured by others. More than half target one or more adults employed by the school. Two-thirds tell someone about their grievance before the attack. Less than one in five threatens his target(s) directly.

- Most attackers are sad before they're angry. Nearly two-thirds have a documented history of extremely depressed or desperate feelings. More than three-quarters have a history of suicidal expressions. Almost all experience or perceive a major loss prior to the attack, and most exhibit considerable difficulty coping.

- Nearly all attackers use guns. Handguns are the most common weapons, followed by rifles and shotguns. Nearly half carry more than one weapon into the attack. Most of the weapons are acquired at the shooter's home or at the home of a relative.

If you're looking for an obvious pattern, there is none. The Secret Service/Department of Education report concludes, "There is no accurate or useful 'profile' of students who engaged in targeted school violence."

By *useful* they mean that adolescent school shooters are typically Caucasian male students who struggle with a self-defined loss and have relatively easy access to a firearm. So we need to keep an eye on roughly one in three American high school kids? That's not very helpful.

Except, of course, it's very useful.

The takeaway here is both simpler and more complicated than almost anyone anticipated: Preventing lethal adolescent violence depends on sustaining attentive relationships with ordinary schoolboys.

It's simple because these guys are in constant contact with adults and peers who are entirely capable of reading the signals of potential violence.

It's complicated because it requires that we take time for deep listening against the backdrop of observable behavior. It's also complicated because it means taking the risk of thinking the unthinkable and speaking the unspeakable.

Preventing violent crime has this in common with preventing suicide: No one wants to think her son is capable of harming himself or others. But he may be. No one enjoys the prospect of asking her son if he's having thoughts about suicide or about taking revenge on someone who caused him harm. But she must.

ACTION PLAN: ENGAGE

- Secure your guns. 30,136 individuals died in 2003 from firearm injuries in the United States—56 percent were completed suicides, 40 percent were homicides, and four percent were accidents.[3] Homes with guns are about five times more likely to experience suicide than homes without guns.[4] From 1976 to 2004, three-quarters of 14-to-17-year-old homicide victims were killed by people using guns.[5] This is not a Constitutional crisis, it's due diligence: If you own guns, secure them and tell your relatives you expect them to do the same.

- Don't frustrate kids needlessly. Consider this ancient wisdom: "Parents, don't come down too hard on your children or you'll crush their spirits" (Colossians 3:21, *The Message*). Perhaps the most common way parents come down too hard on kids is expecting more than children can possibly deliver at their stage of life. Be realistic in your assessment of your child's capabilities. No matter how intelligent or accomplished he is, he's also a teenager and therefore relatively inexperienced and subject to tidal surges of hormones and not yet fully mature in his reasoning and...the list goes on. Instead of coming down hard when your child fails to live up to adult performance standards, bend down a little and meet him where he is. Making a point about what he called *the divine condescension*, C.S. Lewis wrote about how "adult minds (but only the best of them) can descend into sympathy with children."[6] Even as they encourage age-appropriate achievement, effective parents don't come down *on* kids but *to* them and *with* them and *for* them.

- Remember. On our best days, we know what our children feel because we felt it ourselves in a life that may seem long ago and far away but which nonetheless connects us to each other. Remembering requires periodic trips through emotional neighborhoods many of us would just as soon not revisit. But it's worth the journey because that kind of remembering helps us identify with an adolescent's feelings and frame them in a larger context (all without diminishing the immediate circumstances and responsibilities). Sometimes that means holding a kid's feet to the fire; other times it means knowing when to let up and show some mercy.

- Look for signs of depression, desperation, and suicide. Overall, adolescents stand a greater chance of dying by suicide than murder and a *much* greater chance of ending their own lives than ending the lives of others. None of us wishes to lose a child either way. Review sections 4.2 on Anger, 4.3 on Bullying, 4.4 on Cheating—review *everything* in chapter 4.0 of this book—in light of the possibility that a depressed or desperate young man may be a danger to himself or to others.

- Pay attention to self-expression. Over a third of targeted school attackers have expressed themselves in violent writings—poems, essays, or journal entries—prior to their attacks. That's three times as many as those who expressed interest in violent video games and half again as many as expressed interest in violent movies and books.[7] Writers shouldn't be punished for creativity; writers should be able to discuss what they've written in age-appropriate literary terms. Trust your senses. If what a kid says about what he wrote (or drew or sang or painted) doesn't pass the smell test, get some help to sort it out.

- Create safe places. Kids need sanctuaries where they can vent and grieve and gain perspective without having to endure a moralizing sermon. Do what you can to create safe places where your child is immune from danger, judgment, and inhumanity.

JH: Kate may remember this differently, but I don't recall ever arguing at our family table. We played with food, made jokes, told stories, and recounted the adventures and misadventures of the day. We didn't do much problem solving or decision making. And we didn't fight. There are plenty of times and places for solving problems. Our table was a safe place to just *be*.

- All it takes to create a sanctuary for simply *being* together is a conscious decision and a shared agreement. A bedroom, the kitchen table, the front stoop—suit yourselves. Just designate a place where everybody checks their guns at the door. The next step is guiding your child toward other adults, families, and youth groups where safety is the norm. Hint: If you're in a friendship or church where you don't feel safe, chances are your child won't either.

- Keep checking in. The prevention strategy here is engagement. You can't know if your son is depressed or desperate about a real or perceived loss or injustice if you go for days at a time without substantive contact. It's hard; everyone is busy; do it anyway. If you can't come up with anything else, if you're fortunate enough to have a dishwasher, disconnect it and make your son dry while you wash. Do whatever it takes to stay in touch.

5.0

PREVENTION
INSIDE | OUT

Sometimes rocks fall from the sky and there's nothing anyone can do about that except thank God she's alive when the dust settles and try to figure out what to do next.

In other cases, preventive measures are in order. Parents are uniquely positioned to prevent all manner of heartache. This is not to say a parent can head off every disaster, but he can do a lot if he knows how. And the *how of prevention* is much like the *how of intervention*: It's relational and it springs from partnerships with kids, other parents, and schools.

PREVENTION IS PERSONAL

Some kids are more susceptible to crisis because they lack the wisdom to avoid trouble or the resources to recover quickly. Parents can encourage and even build experience and perceptions of personal strength that contribute to refusal skills and post-crisis resilience in their children.

PREVENTION IS RELATIONAL

Arthur C. Clarke, the scientist-novelist-inventor, came by his double-hyphenate status honestly. He wrote *2001: A Space Odyssey*; he also developed the basic theory on which satellite communication technology was launched. And he must have been one of the most frustrated scientists on the planet as the year 2004 drew to a close.

Clarke, who moved to Sri Lanka in 1956, was working with the Japan US Science Technology & Space Applications Program on something called *Project Warn,*[1] a tsunami-warning system for the Asian region (like the systems already in place elsewhere). The system was scheduled for a test in late spring 2005. But that turned out to be several months *after* a 9.0 earthquake disrupted the water off the northwest coast of Sumatra, kicking out two giant waves that surged in a 360-degree pattern killing more than 200,000 people from Indonesia to Somalia.

Clarke knew perhaps better than anyone the limits on satellite detection of tsunamis because those waves *surge* more than *swell*. So there's no obvious surface change to signal what's happening. In this case the water level rose and moved at the speed of a commercial jetliner without generating anything that could be *seen* from above until it was too late to respond.

The *Project Warn* design depends on *proximity*. A network of sensors is spaced across a wide expanse of water to measure change patterns because that's what it takes to detect a tsunami—the sensors have to be in the water.

In crisis intervention *relationship is proximity.* If no one is close enough to sense a disturbance, there's nothing a parent can do to prevent a crisis in a teenager's life. Effective crisis prevention engages a network of friends and caring adults who look out for each other and know each other well enough to sense when something is going wrong.

What sorts of crises can such a network prevent?

- Addiction: By observing and responding to patterns of self-medication, impulsiveness, compulsiveness, suggestibility, and poorly developed refusal skills

- Bullying: By creating safe environments where no one is permitted to harass or demean another

- Codependency: By observing and addressing unhealthy attachments, people pleasing, and rescuing

- Cutting and Self-Mutilation: By observing and responding to anger, frustration, anxiety, victimization, and efforts to cover up or display wounds and scars

- Eating Disorders: By observing and responding to unhealthy body images and unwholesome attitudes toward food

- Running Away or Flight: By observing and responding to patterns of family conflict, frustration, and anxiety

- Sexual Exploitation: By observing and responding to evidence of low self-esteem, eating disorders, or peer-like attachments with much older or much younger people

- Suicide: By sensing and responding to depression, heartbreak, anger, and hopelessness

- Truancy: By observing and responding to poorly developed or declining learning patterns, perceptual difficulties, and a noticeable lack of motivation

- Violence: By observing and responding to signs of victimization, frustration, anger, vandalism, animal cruelty, and self abuse

5.1 INSIDE PREVENTION: **BUILDING RESILIENCE**

Resilience is the capacity to recover quickly from a crisis. Resilient kids spring back from a crisis because they have the internal resources to deal with the world as it is (however far that may be from the world as they would have it).

You can't protect your child from crisis—sometimes the good kids of good parents fall victim to the mistakes and bad behavior of others; sometimes those good kids have accidents, make poor decisions, turn right where they should have turned left; sometimes bad things happen for no apparent reason.

What you *can* do is build resilience in your child.

TAKE KIDS SERIOUSLY

Kids feel discounted most of the time. Their job description consists mainly of waiting for adults to tell them what to do and then waiting for adults to tell them how they did.

Any parent can step out of the pack by taking his child seriously, declaring her essential humanness (and the humanness of her friends too—even if they drive him a little batty sometimes).

This means telling the truth about what sort of world this is—in all its beauty and pain. It means acknowledging that the world isn't a particularly safe place for kids. And pledging to come alongside them no matter what.

Taking teenagers seriously also means inviting them to come alongside us in doing important things. We don't know anyone who regrets bringing their children to serve with them at the soup kitchen or building houses with Habitat for Humanity or becoming Compassion child sponsors.

The United Nations Youth Peer Education Network (Y-PEER) promotes peer-to-peer learning programs in part because:

> Proponents of youth-adult partnerships see young people as individuals with the capacity to make positive and wide-ranging contributions when they receive support and the opportunity to develop their skills. Few things can more concretely demonstrate a belief in young people's capabilities than when trusted adults share with youth the power to make decisions.

> The literature leaves little doubt that youth involvement benefits those youth who participate meaningfully in programmes. By providing young people the opportunity to develop skills, competencies, leadership abilities, self-confidence and self-esteem, youth involvement programmes contribute to building resilience, a protective factor that can help prevent negative health outcomes and risky behaviors.[1]

What's true of effective peer-based experiences is at least equally true of cross-generational experiences: Kids who learn empathy, negotiation, and collaboration become more resilient people.

TEACH HEALTHY SELF-ASSESSMENT

Self-assessment is a skill by which people figure out where they are in the moment. It's global positioning for personal well-being. There are three coordinates:

- How am I doing physically?

- How am I doing emotionally and spiritually?

- How am I doing relationally?

JH: Somebody in the short, illustrious history of Alcoholics Anonymous figured out that recovering addicts are most likely to slip when they're angry, lonely, hungry, or tired. They came up with an acronym to describe those circumstances—HALT—and the shared wisdom: *Don't let yourself get too—*

Hungry

Angry

Lonely

Tired

This marvelously simple tool has gotten me out of more binds than I can recount. The first time I wrote about this, it was pretty fresh:

> A couple of weeks ago I was ready to have it out with everybody in the company. Things were not going like anybody planned. In fact, it was as if nobody had planned at all, which wasn't true, so I was really angry. So angry, in fact, that I paused outside the door I was about to break down. I HALTed out there and asked myself:

- *Am I hungry?* Uh, yeah. I ate about six or seven hours ago. My blood sugar is subterranean.

- *Who am I angry with and why?* Actually, my anger has very little to do with the people in this room. I'm angry with someone in another room who agreed to one thing and then did another and left me holding the bag.

- *Am I lonely?* Yep. I feel totally isolated right now.

- *Am I tired?* Yesterday was very long, last night very short.

All that took about five seconds. I turned around and went to my office, ate a PowerBar, called my wife to chat for a few minutes, thought about what I really wanted to say to the person who bailed on the agreement, and looked at my to-do list to see what could be postponed for a fresh start tomorrow.

That done, I had a brief but pointed discussion with the one I was really mad at, finished a couple of details, turned off the lights, and went home. Much healthier than the drive-by shooting I nearly executed on the rest of the team.

I've taught kids to HALT too. A light came on when I told my friend Brian about HALT. He was having emotional and relational conflicts in his life outside of school. I asked him to describe his afternoon routine: Finish school, drive to work, consume Kit Kats and 20 ounces of Mountain Dew, clock in, and get to work.

"And what happens about 30 minutes after that?" I asked.

"I crash," he said thoughtfully. "I get cranky, and I'm not fit to work with."

"Why do you suppose that is?"

"I think my blood sugar crashes."

"What do you think you could do differently?"

"I could eat smarter," he said and did—the next day and every day since (more or less). And it changed his life.

No kidding. It changed his life the way learning to type changes people's lives. It's not the gift of speech, but it's a potent new tool, a shortcut, a way to improve the utility of the gift.

My modest proposal: Learn to HALT and teach your children.

TEACH A SOPHISTICATED EMOTIONAL VOCABULARY

Most kids inherit an impoverished emotional vocabulary from their parents (who are just passing on what they received from *their* parents). As a consequence, kids are poorly equipped to express themselves clearly. In fact, lacking the language to describe their experiences, they may be baffled by what those experiences even are.

The problem is not new, but the consequences appear to have compounded in recent years. Sex, violence, drunkenness, failure, insult, enthusiasm, excellence, pain—all these have come to be described by one word, and the word rhymes with *buck, cluck, duck, muck,* and *stuck.* It's very nearly the most extreme word in the English language; and because it has come to mean just about everything, it no longer means much of anything.

So there is no language for outrage. If a kid regularly uses our most extreme language in ordinary discourse with his close friends, what then? There's nothing left for his enemies. In the absence of language, what's left but to act out? He'd really better have a gun under the seat of his car, hadn't he?

Parents can teach their adolescents a more sophisticated emotional vocabulary (assuming they acquire one for themselves) and help them learn to use it properly. Kids need to learn the difference between disappointment and frustration, surprise and shock, relief and satisfaction.

> **JH:** A couple of weeks before this writing I was attempting to mediate a complicated family situation when the father said he felt disrespected by the son. I asked him to say more about that disrespected feeling then, still not sure I understood what he was getting at, I asked, "Would you say you feel more *disrespected* or more *betrayed?*"
>
> *Betrayed,* he told me emphatically, then launched into his perceptions of his son's betrayal.
>
> "Lemme ask you this," I said: "Do you feel more *betrayed* or more *let down?*"

His face softened visibly. "Yeah, that's it," he said. "I just feel let down." Then he talked about his disappointment at being lied to repeatedly and intentionally. The man and his son both agreed there's a big difference between feeling *disrespected*, *betrayed*, and *let down*. That wasn't enough to resolve their problem but it was one moment of clarity in a very murky circumstance.

Empowering kids with a rich emotional vocabulary builds resilience by enabling them to identify just how bad things are and to measure their progress before, during, and after a period of crisis. In appendix 6.3 you'll find a list of emotional descriptions to help you and your child describe what you're really feeling and say what you really mean to say.

5.2 OUTSIDE PREVENTION:
BUILDING PREVENTIVE PARTNERSHIPS

PREVENTION SPRINGS FROM PARTNERSHIPS

In most cases, the network of relationships that makes prevention work is natural and obvious to the casual observer. It's a network of parents, friends, and caring adults who are near enough to notice when something goes wrong.

Sometimes that's not enough. Sometimes what's required is a network of intentional partnerships that includes siblings and other kids, teachers, school administrators, and other parents.

- Friends are generally the first to sense signs of struggle

- Siblings often see what parents miss

- Other parents frequently sense when things are upside down in the neighborhood—even if they don't know what to do about it

- Teachers see students often enough to track the ebb and flow of social interaction and emotional well-being

- School administrators can bring focus and urgency to an emerging problem

KIDS AS PREVENTIVE PARTNERS

No one is closer to kids than other kids. It's literally a proximity thing. It's also why mobilizing adolescents to create a preventive community makes so much sense.

Students engage their peers even more than teachers and at *potentially greater* depth across a wider range of life issues than any adult. We say potentially greater, because it's always possible to keep things at the level of video games and pop culture gossip, and plenty of teenagers do just that.

One way to counter that is turning your home into a sanctuary for kids.

Create a Safe Environment

Don't allow anyone to be harassed by anyone else in your home—physically, emotionally, intellectually, socially, or spiritually. Make your home the kind of place that draws your kid's friends because they get unconditional love and acceptance they can't get anywhere else.

Creating a safe home begins when you break the code of silence with your own kids. The code of silence revolves around the pretense that everything is fine when everything is not in fact fine. Some days are wonderful. Some days are better than others. The rest stink. Everyone knows this. When the social norm is pretending no one has any recent failures and nobody is facing anything they can't handle, there's just no way that's a safe home. When you agree to deal with life as it is, rather than life as it's supposed to be, you'll have the opportunity to help young people deal with small problems, rather than hearing about their travails only after the fat hits the fire.

No one can wish a home to safety. Safety is engendered bit by bit through storytelling. Your family is safe when *any* story can be told without fear of retribution—and, perhaps more importantly, with hope of getting help—if that's what's required for a happy ending. That doesn't mean going around the dinner table and putting everyone on the spot every time you're together (which is actually a good motivation for learning to bluff and shade the truth); it means communicating that each one's story is welcome. It means listening compassionately, withholding judgment, and keeping confidence appropriately.

By and large, teenagers know when things are upside down because they suffer everything from psychic stress to weight loss to relational meltdowns. Some kids try to numb their pain with more of what's causing it—like smokers who fire up because their lungs are killing them. It doesn't take long to figure out that's not working. What it takes is a safe place to get a grip on that reality and decide what to do about it. Judgment from you won't speed that up. But honest, inviting questions will: "Is this behavior really working for you? Because you seem miserable (or desperate, manic, out of control, scared, or whatever fits)."

Don't get us wrong: Safety is not about striking an *it's-all-good* pose. It's just that the less you judge, the more adolescents will disclose.

Teach your own kids the practices of deep listening from section 2.4. When they learn to ask good questions and listen well—when your whole family learns to withhold judgment without surrendering wisdom—the result is trust. And out of trust grows safety.

Safe homes make space for silence. If you ask a question and don't get a quick answer, it may mean your child is confused. Or asleep. Or gone. Or the silence may mean the child is thinking. If you can't tell which then ask.

When you create a genuinely safe home, your kids and their friends will become partners in prevention by looking out for each other during all those hours when you're not around.

Cultivate Empathy

Empathy is identifying with what another person feels. Empathy is a standard feature in healthy homes because everyone knows the truth about everyone else. And knowing the truth opens the door to understanding that we're all in it together.

When families get close enough to each other, it turns out no one is better or worse or really all that much different from the rest. This is the oldest lesson in the book. The differences between us are not in the *fact* of our brokenness and wrongdoing but only in the details. It's the old joke from the enormously talented comedian Louie Anderson: Anderson, who has always struggled with his weight, said he saw a picture of a guy who weighed 1,200 pounds. "Twelve hundred pounds!" Anderson mugged, his jowls going slack. "Now *that* guy has a weight problem!"

In the empathetic home, family members stop trying to divert attention from their weakness by pointing out the weaknesses of others. The result is ever-increasing safety.

It's probably not a wild assumption to guess that most kids get lost on the emotional map once they step beyond their comfort zone. Since empathy involves identifying with another person's emotions, it's good to have a shared language. Use the emotional map in appendix 6.3 to help your kid build an empathic vocabulary.

Peer Intervention and Referral

You can teach adolescents the art of crisis intervention. Mostly this kind of intervention won't be called *intervention*; it will be called *friendship*.

Help your youngsters learn that calling someone a *friend* means more than, *I like you*. Friendship is a commitment to look out for the best interests of another person. That means helping her get what she wants—unless what she wants is clearly not what she needs. It means making it difficult for her to engage in self-destructive behavior. It means asking tough questions when she gets too big for her britches.

If an enemy is someone who stabs you in the back, a friend is someone who stabs you in the front, surgically holding you accountable to get the help you need to keep growing. Help your children understand that a friend does this not because he's *better* than them but because he's so nearly *the same*. Teach your kids the principles of *intervention* in section 3.3.

Then you can teach them to go get help for a friend when they're both in over their heads. Asking for help is hard for young people for the same reasons it's hard for adults: Pride, fear, ambition, wishful thinking, and who knows what else? Help your kids learn to let go by helping them understand there's no failure in admitting their friend needs more than they can deliver—just as there's nothing heroic about keeping it to themselves once they have reason to believe their friend is in deep trouble. Remember: *It's not about me; it's not about me; it's not about me.*

Speaking of which, you may not be the best person to help your child's friend. In addition to you, help your child identify another competent adult—a youth worker or teacher or staff member at school—who's most likely to pitch in fast if needed. Give them the Boys and Girls Town National Hotline number—800-448-3000—as a go-to resource in a pinch. (They're not just knowledgeable about defusing emotional time bombs; the hotline also has a terrific database of helping resources in every area code.)

OTHER PARENTS AS PARTNERS

It's true that some parents are clueless at best, malevolent at worst, but most parents mean well. (Those who don't mean well are in a special class reserved for psychopaths and the evil—you're not likely to meet many of them.)

Most parents do the best they can under the circumstances. Those circumstances may include mediocre to lousy preparation for parenthood, occupational and financial stress, personal unhappiness, weakness, brokenness, distraction, addiction, confusion, misinformation, fatigue, anxiety, immaturity, poor relational skills, and spiritual rootlessness—in addition to the naïveté, arrogance, fear, ambition, and wishful thinking we've seen from time to time in our own mirrors.

At our best and our worst, all parents are human with all the positive and negative characteristics associated with that blessedly maddening condition.

Some parents view their children with contempt but most do not.

Some parents are relentlessly self-absorbed but most are not.

Some parents are unreasonable but most are not.

This means most parents can be your partner in prevention—if only because they have the proximity to pay attention to the kids who pass through their doors. Far beyond that, a lot of parents are looking for partners to help them in the task that's uniquely theirs: Preparing their children to be women and men.

Here are four ways to engage other parents as partners in prevention:

1. Reality check. If you think something may be out of balance with a kid, check with his parents...*discreetly*. Don't alarm them and don't create suspicion; just ask how he's doing. If they want to know why you're asking, say you're not sure. Tell them something just feels slightly off when he's over at your place and you wondered if it was just you. If you *are* sure something isn't right, maybe you should start the conversation with a statement about that conviction (rather than a question that might be viewed as a setup).

If the parents seem worked up by your question, remind them that episodic short-term depression, anxiety, anger, attention deficit, fatigue, weight fluctuation, and general goofiness are all pretty common in adolescence and nothing to be distressed about. Reassure them you're not meddling or projecting—just checking on the well-being of a terrific kid.

2. Early warning. Ask other parents what teenagers, moms, and dads are talking about around the neighborhood. Your subcultural awareness may alert you to something another adult would miss. This notion is borrowed from the study of epidemics in which clus-

tered health events may be an early warning of a larger public concern.[1] They're usually not, but they can be.

For instance, if your casual questioning turns up references to an unexpected number of fights, pregnancies, eating disorders, runaways, hospitalizations, car accidents, or exploding trailer homes, then that may tip you off to an increase in sexual activity, drinking, or the arrival of a new drug in your community; or it may signal an uptick in rage or gang activity. As in medicine, such clusters usually turn out to be coincidental and unrelated; but every once in a while, they point to something significant.

3. Networkers. There are folks in your network of parents who can introduce you to people you need to know in the larger community of schools, churches, hospitals, and law enforcement. Don't use the phone book when you can get a qualified recommendation from someone you know.

4. Innkeepers. There will come a time when you need to arrange a few nights' lodging for a kid or a spouse—your own or somebody else's—who needs a time-out from the household. There are other parents who can give you a yes on that in real time.

The only things that can prevent you from engaging other parents as partners in prevention are your own pride, fear, shortsightedness, or inertia (sometimes experienced as laziness).

Consider developing a peer-to-peer learning and support network. We're partial to a process called *Developing Capable People.*[2] Get training for yourself and a couple of parents and go to town.

PREVENTIVE PARTNERSHIPS WITH SCHOOLS

If we hear one more person-who-ought-to-know-better bad-mouth teachers, there's gonna be trouble. Nobody has more contact with students than teachers. School administrators and staff are right behind them. Does anybody think they're in it for the money? Or the short workday? *Puh-leeze!*

There are exceptions, and parts of the system are broken; but most of the teachers we know are dedicated to students and they're surprised and hurt when their devotion is questioned. The same goes for administrators and staff, most of whom are committed professionals. That makes them natural allies once it's clear you share their commitments.

Appendix 6.7 is a glossary of terms common in community and school-based prevention and intervention programs (which have about as many abbreviations and about as much jargon as anything you'll find). So be patient when you come in contact with those folks; ask for clarification when you don't know what they're talking about and keep this book handy so you can look up terms you didn't quite catch while you're still able to remember the words and abbreviations you heard.

Consider aligning yourself with a community-based organization dedicated to helping schools. Look for local chapters of Parents for Drug-Free Youth or the National Family Partnership or Mothers Against Drunk Driving or whatever the equivalents are called in your community. These organizations are always in need of fresh blood.

After you've gone to a few meetings—and done a lot of thoughtful listening—do something many people in such groups never think to do: Tell them you'd like to visit with a couple of site administrators to see how they feel about their prevention programs and resources.

Assuming this isn't a problem for anyone, ask your children and their friends which school administrators have a reputation for caring about kids, then make an appointment with at least one of those individuals for a brief meeting to introduce yourself and ask on behalf of your community organization what they wish they had for prevention and intervention at their site. In the initial meeting:

- Explain that you have no agenda other than to find out what they're doing about prevention and intervention on the campus and what they wish they had to help them do a better job. If they seem to suspect you have a hidden agenda, it's not you; it's someone who came before you with an axe to grind or something to sell.

- Promise to report your conversation to the community organization you're aligned with—ask if there's anything from the conversation that the administrator wishes you *wouldn't* include in your verbal report.

- Listen more than you talk.

- Make a faithful and generous report to your community group and, if you can, help the school get what it needs to take better care of its students.

The least that's likely to come from this kind of interaction is that you'll know someone at school if you ever need help there. And that's not a bad thing.

5.3 A FINAL **WORD**

RVP: *Tim was born last in a family with three children. I always thought his stay-at-home mom and M.D. dad would easily qualify for the Ward & June Cleaver Invitational Parenting Tournament— totally immersed in the church, the school, the community, and the lives of their children.*

Except for one thing. They missed that Tim was a closet alcoholic. In fairness, it should be said he concealed it carefully throughout high school. No one knew that by his senior year he needed a little something first thing in the morning to jumpstart the day. It's not even clear that his peers were aware he drank between classes to take the edge off. That's some pretty good hiding.

And alcohol more or less worked for Tim, right into his sophomore year in college when a police officer pulled him over for a broken turn signal and smelled booze on his breath. Even then Tim's tolerance for alcohol enabled him to walk a straight line. But the breathalizer gave him away; his blood-alcohol level clocking many times over the legal limit.

You can imagine the shock and parental shame that The Beaver grew up to be a drunk. But as much as Tim's mom and dad wanted to deny the severity of his condition, as much as they longed to protect the family name and their son's reputation, they made the tough decision to place him in a residential treatment program against his will.

It was a messy recovery. Months of treatment, interrupted by multiple relapses, tested their resolve. Then Tim enlisted in the armed forces and was out of their custody. But he was not beyond their loving engagement; they never gave up on him, and somewhere along the line, it clicked for Tim.

After he mustered out of the military, Tim returned to college— then continued to medical school. Tim is in his 30s now and a family man himself. I'm happy to report he gets along well with his parents; in fact, Tim recently took over his dad's medical practice.

JH: It was not yet dawn when my friend found his 17 year-old on her bedroom floor. She'd carved a cross on her chest—or was it an X?—and emptied a bottle of pills. Nearby lay an empty ice cream carton...a final indulgence as she loosed her grip on life. I knew her well. She was racked by an eating disorder about which we spoke endlessly and without much effect. I never knew her to think straight about her body image or the meaning of food.

So she was surprised to wake up in the hospital—she hadn't intended to wake up at all. In those first touch-and-go days her dad said something that expressed the magnitude of the change they were undertaking. "None of the dreams I had for her matter," he told me, "what matters is she's alive."

The next couple of years were singularly difficult. At the beginning, she spent her days—including several intense weeks in treatment programs *rethinking...**everything***. She didn't go to Prom; she didn't walk with her class at graduation; she didn't leave for college in the fall; she didn't fulfill the considerable promise of her upper-middle-class life.

And it turned out none of that mattered.

Today she's more than merely alive; she's *living*. She's in her mid-30s; married to a man she loves and who loves her; the mom of two beautiful schoolboys; and good friends with her mom and dad...all things that seemed impossible the night she swallowed pills, ate a carton of ice cream, and lost consciousness.

We write about crisis because we have hope. We have so many adult friends whose lives, when we knew them as adolescents, could have gone either way; who took a turn for the better in large part because their parents stood by them, supported them, and gave them a sense of hope when they had nowhere to turn. We have even more friends who, though we didn't know them as kids, tell similar tales.

Parents are often the heroes of these stories because when the chips are down, parents so often surrender their dreams and come alongside to help adolescents as they *are*—not as they're supposed to be. This is generally not about fairy-tale endings; it's usually about recovery; picking up the pieces; sadder-but-wiser girls and boys; making the best of a bad thing; walking with a limp.

And there's nothing wrong with that. In a perfect world there would be, but God knows this ain't no perfect world. "Man is born broken," Eugene O'Neill writes. "He lives by mending. The grace of God is glue."

We know a thing or two about mending. In fact we have come to depend on *do-overs*—we don't know anyone who doesn't need them in steady supply, beginning with us. If we two have any capacity for understanding and showing mercy, it's only because understanding and mercy have been extended to us over and over and over again by the people closest to us and—we believe—by the Creator who loves us and gave himself for us.[1]

So we have hope. We've experienced the dangerous opportunity of crisis for ourselves, and we are no longer afraid.

Well, okay, we're still afraid sometimes. C.S. Lewis wasn't exactly giddy with anticipation when he wrote to a friend: "We are not necessarily doubting that God will do the best for us; we are wondering how painful the best will turn out to be."[2]

We wouldn't know how to say it any better than that. We embrace the painful best—for our children and ourselves—because we have come to believe the God we trust does not waste pain.

Hemingway has a character say, "The world breaks everyone," and there is no argument about this. Generation after generation on every land mass, the record of humankind is a tragic litany of brokenness. But that record isn't without its tales of redemption and hope reborn. So it's the second part of Hemingway's line that we invite you celebrate with us—even if we must celebrate somewhat cautiously: "The world breaks everyone," Hemingway says, "and afterwards many are strong at the broken places."[3]

Our hope for you and us and the kids we care for is that we all get what we need to grow strong at the broken places. That's the promise of dangerous opportunity.

6.0

APPENDICES

6.1 ACTION PLAN **WORKSHEET**

I.   What is the identified problem (beyond the presenting problem)?

II. What are the possible outcomes (both negative and positive)?

   A. Which is the most desirable outcome?

   B. What general steps are required to move toward that outcome? (Return to more specific steps later.)

III. Who are the active participants, and what is their stake in the outcome?

IV. Who are the passive participants, and what is their stake?

   (And what can be expected from each stakeholder?)

V.   What are the resources and roadblocks to reaching the goal?

VI. Who else should be involved in the solution?

    A. Extended family?

    B. Professional referral?

        1. Medical doctor?

        2. Psychiatrist, psychologist?

        3. Social worker?

        4. Law enforcement?

        5. Lawyer?

        6. Pastor, youth worker?

        7. School personnel?

        8. Employer?

        9. Friends?

VII. What specific steps must be taken?

    A. In what order?

    B. Who should take responsibility for each step?

    C. Who should provide support?

VIII. What is the timetable?

IX. What other resources are required?

    A. Money?

    B. Transportation?

    C. Temporary lodging?

D. Food?

E. Other?

X. Who will provide ongoing support and feedback?

6.2 CHILD ABUSE **REPORTING NUMBERS**

Each state designates specific agencies to receive and investigate reports of suspected child abuse and neglect. Typically, this responsibility is carried out by Child Protective Services (CPS) within a Department of Social Services, Department of Human Resources, or Division of Family and Children Services. In some states, police departments may also receive reports of child abuse or neglect.

For more information or assistance with reporting, call Childhelp® USA, 800-4-A-CHILD (800-422-4453), or your local CPS agency.

In most cases, the toll-free numbers listed below are only accessible from within the state listed. If calling from out-of-state, use the local (toll) number listed or call Childhelp® USA for assistance.

Also listed below are links to state Web sites, which can provide additional information. *(These results are current as of June 2007.)*

Alabama
Local (toll): (334) 242-9500
Web site: *http://www.dhr.state.al.us/page.asp?pageid=304*

Alaska
Toll-free: (800) 478-4444
Web site: *http://www.hss.state.ak.us/ocs/default.htm*

Arizona
Toll-free: (888) SOS-CHILD (888-767-2445)
Web site: *http://www.de.state.az.us/dcyf/cps/*

Arkansas
Toll-free: (800) 482-5964
Web site: *http://www.state.ar.us/dhs/chilnfam/child_protective_services.htm*

California
Web site: *http://www.dss.cahwnet.gov/cdssweb/ChildAbuse_188.htm*

Colorado
Local (toll): (303) 866-5932
Web site: *http://www.cdhs.state.co.us/childwelfare/index.htm*

Connecticut
TDD: (800) 624-5518
Toll-free: (800) 842-2288
Web site: *http://www.ct.gov/dcf/site/default.asp*

Delaware
Toll-free: (800) 292-9582
Web site: http://kids.delaware.gov/services/crisis.shtml

District of Columbia
Toll-free: (877) 671-SAFE (877-671-7233)
Local (toll): (202) 671-7233
Web site: *http://cfsa.dc.gov/cfsa/cwp/view.asp?a=3&q=520663&cfsaNav=|31319|*

Florida
Toll-free: (800) 96-ABUSE (800-962-2873)
Web site: *http://www.dcf.state.fl.us/abuse/*

Georgia

Web site: *http://dfcs.dhr.georgia.gov/portal/site*

Contact local agency or Childhelp USA for assistance.

Hawaii

Local (toll): (808) 832-5300

Web site: *http://www.hawaii.gov/dhs/protection/social_services/child_welfare/*

Idaho

TDD: (208) 332-7205

Toll-free: (800) 926-2588

Web site: *http://www.healthandwelfare.idaho.gov/site/3333/default.aspx*

Illinois

Toll-free: (800) 252-2873

Local (toll): (217) 785-4020

Web site: *http://www.state.il.us/dcfs/child/index.shtml*

Indiana

Toll-free: (800) 800-5556

Web site: *http://www.in.gov/dcs/protection/dfcchi.html*

Iowa

Toll-free: (800) 362-2178

Web site: *http://www.dhs.state.ia.us/dhs2005/dhs_homepage/children_family/abuse_reporting/child_abuse.html*

Kansas

Toll-free: (800) 922-5330

Local (toll): (785) 296-0044

Web site: *http://www.srskansas.org/services/child_protective_services.htm*

Kentucky

Toll-free: (800) 752-6200

Local (toll): (502) 595-4550

Web site: *http://chfs.ky.gov/dcbs/dpp/childsafety.htm*

Louisiana

Local (toll): (225) 342-6832

Web site: *http://www.dss.state.la.us/departments/ocs/Reporting_Child_Abuse-Neglect.html*

Maine

Toll-free: (800) 452-1999

Web site: *http://www.maine.gov/dhhs/bcfs/abusereporting.htm*

Maryland

Toll-free: (800) 332-6347

Web site: *http://www.dhr.state.md.us/cps/report.htm*

Massachusetts

Toll-free: (800) 792-5200

Web site: *http://www.mass.gov/?pageID=eohhs2subtopic&L=5&L0=Home&L1=Consumer&L2=Family+Services&L3=Violence%2c+Abuse+or+Neglect&L4=Child+Abuse+and+Neglect&sid=Eeohhs2*

Michigan

Toll-free: (800) 942-4357

Local (toll): (517) 373-3572

Web site: *http://www.michigan.gov/dhs/0,1607,7-124-5452_7119---,00.html*

Minnesota

Local (toll): (651) 291-0211

Web site: *http://www.dhs.state.mn.us/main/idcplg?IdcService=GET_DYNAM-IC_CONVERSION&RevisionSelectionMethod=LatestReleased&dDocName=id_000152*

Mississippi
Toll-free: (800) 222-8000
Local (toll): (601) 359-4991
Web site: *http://www.mdhs.state.ms.us/fcs_prot.html*

Missouri
Toll-free: (800) 392-3738
Local (toll): (573) 751-3448
Web site: *http://www.dss.mo.gov/cd/rptcan.htm*

Montana
Toll-free: (866) 820-KIDS (866-820-5437)
Local (toll): (406) 444-5900
Web site: *http://www.dphhs.mt.gov/cfsd/index.shtml*

Nebraska
Toll-free: (800) 652-1999
Local (toll): (402) 595-1324
Web site: *http://www.hhs.state.ne.us/cha/chaindex.htm*

Nevada
Toll-free: (800) 992-5757
Local (toll): (775) 684-4400
Web site: *http://dcfs.state.nv.us/DCFS_PhDirectory.htm*

New Hampshire
Toll-free: (800) 894-5533
Local (toll): (603) 271-6556
Web site: *http://www.dhhs.state.nh.us/DHHS/BCP/default.htm*

New Jersey
TDD: (800) 835-5510
Toll-free: (877) 652-2873
Web site: *http://www.state.nj.us/dcf/divisions/dyfs/hotlines.html*

New Mexico
Toll-free: (800) 797-3260
Local (toll): (505) 841-6100
Web site: *http://www.cyfd.org/index.htm*

New York
TDD: (800) 369-2437
Toll-free: (800) 342-3720
Local (toll): (518) 474-8740
Web site: *http://www.ocfs.state.ny.us/main/cps/*

North Carolina
Web site: *http://www.dhhs.state.nc.us/dss/cps/index.htm*
Contact local agency or Childhelp USA for assistance.

North Dakota
Local (toll): (701) 328-2316
Web site: *http://www.nd.gov/humanservices/services/childfamily/cps/*

Ohio
Web site: *http://jfs.ohio.gov/county/cntydir.stm*
Contact local agency or Childhelp USA for assistance.

Oklahoma
Toll-free: (800) 522-3511
Web site: *http://www.okdhs.org/programsandservices/cps/*

Oregon
TDD: (503) 378-5414
Toll-free: (800) 854-3508; Ext. 2402
Local (toll): (503) 378-6704
Web site: *http://www.oregon.gov/DHS/children/abuse/cps/report.shtml*

Pennsylvania
Toll-free: (800) 932-0313
Web site: *http://www.dpw.state.pa.us/Child/ChildAbuseNeglect/*

Rhode Island
Toll-free: (800) RI-CHILD (800-742-4453)
Web site: *http://www.dcyf.ri.gov/child_welfare/index.php*

South Carolina
Local (toll): (803) 898-7318
Web site: *http://www.state.sc.us/dss/cps/index.html*

South Dakota
Local (toll): (605) 773-3227
Web site: *http://dss.sd.gov/cps/protective/reporting.asp*

Tennessee
Toll-free: (877) 237-0004
Web site: *http://state.tn.us/youth/childsafety.htm*

Texas
Toll-free: (800) 252-5400
Web site: *http://www.dfps.state.tx.us/Child_Protection/About_Child_Protective_Services/reportChildAbuse.asp*

Utah
Toll-free: (800) 678-9399
Web site: *http://www.hsdcfs.utah.gov*

Vermont
After hours: (800) 649-5285
Web site: *http://www.dcf.state.vt.us/fsd/reporting/index.html*

Virginia

Toll-free: (800) 552-7096

Local (toll): (804) 786-8536

Web site: *http://www.dss.virginia.gov/family/cps/index.html*

Washington

Toll-free: (866) END-HARM (866-363-4276)

Web site: *http://www1.dshs.wa.gov/ca/safety/abuseReport.asp?2*

West Virginia

Toll-free: (800) 352-6513

Web site: *http://www.wvdhhr.org/bcf/children_adult/cps/report.asp*

Wisconsin

Local (toll): (608) 266-3036

Web site: *http://www.dhfs.state.wi.us/Children/CPS/cpswimap.HTM*

Wyoming

Web site: *http://dfsweb.state.wy.us/ProtectiveSvc/programs/cps/Report.htm*

Contact local agency or Childhelp USA for assistance.

Information courtesy of the National Clearinghouse on Child Abuse and Neglect Information— *http://www.childwelfare.gov/pubs/reslist/rl_dsp.cfm?rs_id=5&rate_chno=11-11172*

6.3 EMOTIONAL **MAP**

Happy
Accepted
Appreciated
Approved Of
Blissful
Calm
Capable
Carefree
Cheerful
Comfortable
Confident
Content
Delighted
Ecstatic
Elated
Encouraged
Enthusiastic
Exhilarated
Exultant
Giddy
Glad
Gleeful
Grateful
High
Hilarious

Hopeful
Inspired
Jolly
Joyous
Knocked Out
Light
Lighthearted
Like a Contributor
Lively
Loved
Merry
Mirthful
Needed
Obnoxious
Optimistic
Overjoyed
Peaceful
Playful
Pleased
Rapturous
Satisfied
Secure
Serene
Significant
Spirited

Sunny
Thankful
Thrilled
Tranquil
Understood
Warm

Unhappy
Bored
Bothered
Cheerless
Choked Up
Cloudy
Dark
Dejected
Depressed
Despondent
Disappointed
Discontent
Discouraged
Disheartened
Distracted
Downcast
Downhearted
Dreadful

Dreary
Dull
Gloomy
Glum
Held Captive
Insignificant
Joyless
Melancholy
Moody
Mopey
Mournful
Oppressed
Out of Sorts
Quiet
Sad
Somber
Sorrowful
Spiritless
Sulky
Sullen
Upset
Vacant
Woeful

Angry
Annoyed
Belligerent
Bent Out of Shape
Bitter
Boiling
Bugged
Contemptuous
Defiant
Disgusted
Enraged
Exasperated

Fuming
Furious
Incensed
Indignant
Inflamed
Infuriated
Irate
Irritated
Mad
Peeved
Perturbed
Riled
Seething
Ticked Off
Touchy
Up in Arms
Worked Up
Wrathful

Hurt
Abandoned
Accused
Aching
Afflicted
Agonized
Belittled
Betrayed
Defensive
Degraded
Deprived
Diminished
Discounted
Disrespected
Grieved
Hampered
Infuriated

Injured
In Pain
Knifed in the Back
Left Out
Let Down
Misused
Offended
Pathetic
Persecuted
Provoked
Put Down
Resentful
Taken Advantage Of
Tortured
Unappreciated
Unimportant
Unloved
Untrusted
Used
Victimized
Woeful
Worried

Overwhelmed
Astounded
Beat
Bewildered
Blah
Blown Away
Broken
Burned Out
Cold
Confused
Crushed
Deflated
Demotivated

Disoriented
Dull
Dumbfounded
Empty
Exhausted
Flat
Floored
Fried
Grief-stricken
Heartbroken
Helpless
Hollow
Humble
Humiliated
In Despair
In Over My Head
Inconsolable
Insecure
Like Giving Up
Like I'm Drowning
Like Quitting
Like Running Away
Low
Lost
Miserable
Mortified
Mournful
Nauseated
Numb
Panicky
Paralyzed
Pessimistic
Plagued
Powerless
Reverent
Shook

Shut Down
Sick
Staggered
Stumped
Stunned
Tired
Weary
Worn Out

Excited
Bold
Brave
Calm
Certain
Confident
Determined
Fearless
Firm
Hungry
Impatient
Resolved
Seductive
Self-reliant
Sexy
Strong

Anxious
Absorbed
Agitated
Alone
Apprehensive
Cautious
Concerned
Curious
Dependent
Distant

Distressed
Distrustful
Doubtful
Eager
Engrossed
Fascinated
Hesitant
Indecisive
Inquisitive
Intent
Interested
Intrigued
Itchy
Nosey
Perplexed
Questioning
Skeptical
Snoopy
Suspicious
Unbelieving
Uncertain
Uneasy
Uptight
Wavering

Afraid
Aghast
Alarmed
Appalled
Apprehensive
Awed
Cautious
Chicken
Cowardly
Dismayed
Fainthearted

Fearful
Fidgety
Frightened
Hesitant
Horrified
Hysterical
Immobilized
Insecure
Lonely
Nervous
Panicky
Paralyzed
Petrified
Restless
Scared
Shaky
Sheepish
Suspicious
Terrified
Threatened
Timid
Trembly

Guilty
Ashamed
Bad
Dumb
Embarrassed
Foolish
Incompetent
Infantile
Like a Failure
Like a Fool
Naïve
Remorseful
Repentant

Ridiculous
Self-conscious
Selfish
Silly
Slow
Stupid
Unfit
Useless
Weird
Worthless
Wrong

Sympathetic
Compassionate
Concerned
Connected
Empathetic
Moved
Understanding

6.4 FIRST AID FOR **AN OVERDOSE**

We hope you never need this. But if you do, a working knowledge of first aid can mean the difference between life and death.

- If the person is conscious, do not allow her to go to sleep. Keep her talking and as alert as possible. Find out what drug(s) were taken and in what quantity.

- If the person is unconscious or comatose, check breathing. Be certain that the throat is clear of foreign matter. Check the body for any necklace, bracelet, or emergency medical card identifying a medical condition that could cause the symptoms you're seeing. Otherwise, check for bottles, pill containers, or any other evidence of what might have been swallowed or injected. Ask friends who might know but are afraid to respond for fear that they might get in trouble.

- If you're able to identify what was ingested or injected and a phone is nearby, call either 911, the poison control center, or a local hospital and ask for instructions about what to do next. If you don't have access to a telephone and can get to help in a relatively short period of time, do not induce vomiting.

- If the person is conscious and has taken the overdose within a two-hour period, dilute the poison or drugs in the stomach with two or three cups of water and induce vomiting. If the overdose was injected, cleaning out the stomach will be of little help.

- Get the person to the nearest hospital or emergency clinic as soon and as safely as possible. Bring any empty bottles or containers of the drugs you suspect were taken.

- Be sure another person, besides the driver, rides along to the hospital so he can provide assistance if the person who overdosed should vomit and also monitor her breathing.

6.5 STATE SEX OFFENDER **REGISTRIES**

The following Web site information was found at http://www.fbi.gov/hq/cid/cac/states.htm. All Web site addresses are current as of June 2007.

Alabama

http://community.dps.state.al.us/

Alaska

http://www.dps.state.ak.us/sorweb/Sorweb.aspx

Arizona

https://az.gov/webapp/offender/main.do

Arkansas

http://www.acic.org/Registration/index.htm

California

http://meganslaw.ca.gov/index.htm

Colorado

http://sor.state.co.us/

Connecticut

http://www.ct.gov/dps/cwp/view.asp?a=2157&Q=294474&dpsNav=|

Delaware

http://www.state.de.us/dsp/sexoff/

District of Columbia

http://mpdc.dc.gov/mpdc/cwp/view,a,1241,Q,540704,mpdcNav_GID,1523,mpdcNav,|,.asp

Florida

http://offender.fdle.state.fl.us/offender/homepage.do

Georgia

http://services.georgia.gov/gbi/gbisor/disclaim.html

Hawaii

http://sexoffenders.hawaii.gov/

Idaho

http://www.isp.state.id.us/identification/sex_offender/

Illinois

http://www.isp.state.il.us/sor/

Indiana

http://www.insor.org/insasoweb/

Iowa

http://www.iowasexoffender.com

Kansas

http://www.accesskansas.org/kbi/ro.shtml

Kentucky

http://kspsor.state.ky.us

Louisiana
http://lasocpr1.lsp.org/

Maine
http://sor.informe.org/sor/

Maryland
http://www.dpscs.state.md.us/onlineservs/sor/

Massachusetts
http://www.mass.gov/?pageID=eopsagencylanding&L=3&L0=Home &L1=Publi c+Safety+Agencies&L2=Sex+Offender+Registry+Board+(SORB)&sid=Eeops

Michigan
http://www.mipsor.state.mi.us/

Minnesota
http://www.dps.state.mn.us/bca/Invest/Documents/Page-07.html

Mississippi
http://www.sor.mdps.state.ms.us/sorpublic/hpsor_search.aspx

Missouri
http://www.mshp.dps.missouri.gov/MSHPWeb/PatrolDivisions/CRID/SOR/SOR-Page.html

Montana
http://doj.mt.gov/svor/

Nebraska
http://www.nsp.state.ne.us/sor/

Nevada
http://www.nvsexoffenders.gov/sorstart.aspx

New Hampshire
http://www.egov.nh.gov/nsor/

New Jersey
http://www.njsp.org/info/reg_sexoffend.html

New Mexico
http://www.nmsexoffender.dps.state.nm.us/servlet/hit_serv.class

New York
http://www.criminaljustice.state.ny.us/nsor/

North Carolina
http://ncfindoffender.com/

North Dakota
http://www.sexoffender.nd.gov/

Ohio
http://www.esorn.ag.state.oh.us/Secured/p1.aspx

Oklahoma
http://docapp8.doc.state.ok.us/servlet/page?_pageid=190&_dad=portal30&_schema=PORTAL30

Oregon
http://sexoffenders.oregon.gov/

Pennsylvania
http://www.pameganslaw.state.pa.us/

Rhode Island
http://www.paroleboard.ri.gov/sexoffender/agree.php

South Carolina
http://services.sled.sc.gov/sor/

South Dakota
http://sor.sd.gov/disclaimer.asp?page=search&nav=2

Tennessee
http://www.ticic.state.tn.us/SEX_ofndr/search_short.asp

Texas
https://records.txdps.state.tx.us/DPS_WEB/Sor/index.aspx

Utah
http://www.udc.state.ut.us/asp-bin/sexoffendersearchform.asp

Vermont
http://170.222.24.9/cjs/s_registry.htm

Virginia
http://sex-offender.vsp.virginia.gov/sor/

Washington
http://ml.waspc.org/Accept.aspx?ReturnUrl=/index.aspx

West Virginia
http://www.wvstatepolice.com/sexoff/

Wisconsin
http://offender.doc.state.wi.us/public/

Wyoming
http://attorneygeneral.state.wy.us/dci/so/so_registration.html

Individual FBI Field Offices serve as primary points of contact for persons re-questing FBI assistance. For further information about FBI services or to request assistance, please contact a Crimes Against Children Coordinator at your local FBI Field Office.

6.6 THE SERENITY **PRAYER**

God, grant me the serenity
to accept the things I cannot change,
courage to change the things I can,
and wisdom to know the difference.

Living one day at a time,
enjoying one moment at a time;
accepting hardships as the pathway to peace;
taking, as He did,
this sinful world as it is,
not as I would have it;
trusting that He will make all things right
if I surrender to His will;
that I may be reasonably happy in this life
and supremely happy
with Him forever in the next.

— attributed to Reinhold Niebuhr

6.7 GLOSSARY OF **CHILD PROTECTIVE SERVICES TERMS**

Acid: Common street name for LSD (Lysergic Acid Diethylamide).

Addiction: A chronic, relapsing disease characterized by compulsive drug seeking and abuse and by long-lasting chemical changes in the brain.

Adjudicatory Hearings: Held by the juvenile and family court to determine whether a child has been maltreated or whether another legal basis exists for the state to intervene to protect the child.

Adoption and Safe Families Act (ASFA): Designed to improve the safety of children, to promote adoption and other permanent homes for children who need them, and to support families. The law requires CPS agencies to provide more timely and focused assessment and intervention services to the children and families that are served within the CPS system.

Adoptive Parent: A person with the legal relation of parent to a child not related by birth, with the same mutual rights and obligations that exist between children and their birth parents. The legal relationship has been finalized.

Age: Age calculated in years at the time of the report of abuse or neglect or as of December 31 of the reporting year.

Alleged Perpetrator: An individual who is alleged to have caused or knowingly allowed the maltreatment of a child as stated in an incident of child abuse or neglect.

Alleged Victim: Child about whom a report regarding maltreatment has been made to a CPS agency.

Alternative Response System: A maltreatment disposition system used in some states that provides for responses other than substantiated, indicated, and unsubstantiated. In such a system, children may or may not be determined to be maltreatment victims. Such a system may be known as a "diversified" system or an "in need of services" system.

Amphetamines: Stimulant drugs whose effects are very similar to cocaine.

Anabolic Steroids: Synthetic substances related to the male sex hormone, which promote the growth of skeletal muscle and the development of male sexual characteristics.

Analgesics: A group of medications that reduce pain.

Angel Dust: Common street name for PCP (Phencyclidine).

Anonymous or Unknown Report Source: An individual who notifies a CPS agency of suspected child maltreatment without identifying himself; or the type of report source is unknown.

Assessment: A process by which the CPS agency determines whether the child or other persons involved in the report of alleged maltreatment are in need of services.

Barbiturate: A type of central nervous system (CNS) depressant often pre-scribed to promote sleep.

Benzodiazepine: A type of CNS depressant prescribed to relieve anxiety; among the most widely prescribed medications, including Valium and Librium.

Biological Parent: The birth mother or father of the child.

Birth Cohort: A birth cohort consists of all persons born within a given period of time, such as a calendar year.

Boy: A male child younger than 18 years old.

Cannabis: The botanical name for the plant from which marijuana comes.

CAPTA: *See Child Abuse Prevention and Treatment Act.*

Caregiver: A person responsible for the care and supervision of the alleged child victim.

CASA: *See Court-Appointed Special Advocate.*

Case-Level Data: Information submitted by the states in the child file containing individual child or report maltreatment characteristics.

Caseworker: A staff person assigned to a report of child maltreatment at the time of the report disposition.

Child: A person younger than 18 years old or considered to be a minor under state law.

Child Abuse and Neglect State Grant: Funding to the states for programs serving abused and neglected children, awarded under the Child Abuse Prevention and Treatment Act (CAPTA). May be used to assist states in intake and assessment, screening and investigation of child abuse and neglect reports, improving risk and safety assessment protocols, training child protective service workers and mandated reporters and improving services to disabled infants with life-threatening conditions.

Child Abuse Prevention and Treatment Act (CAPTA) [42 U.S.C. 5101 et seq.]: Law that provides the foundation for federal involvement in child protection and child welfare services. The 1996 Amendments provide for, among other things, annual state data reports on child maltreatment to the Secretary of Health and Human Services.

Child Daycare Provider: A person with a temporary caregiver responsibility, but who is not related to the child, such as a daycare center staff member, a family daycare provider, or a baby-sitter. Does not include persons with legal custody or guardianship of the child.

Child Death Review Team: A state team of professionals who reviews all reports surrounding the death of a child.

Child Maltreatment: An act or failure to act by a parent, caregiver, or other person as defined under state law that results in physical abuse, neglect, medical neglect, sexual abuse, emotional abuse, or an act or failure to act that presents an imminent risk of serious harm to a child.

Child Protective Services (CPS): An official agency of a state having the responsibility for child protective services and activities. CPS receives reports, investigates, and provides intervention and treatment services to children and families in which child maltreatment has occurred. Frequently, this agency is located within larger public social service agencies, such as the Department of Social Services.

Child Protective Services (CPS) Supervisor: The manager of the caseworker assigned to a report of child maltreatment at the time of the report disposition.

Child Protective Services (CPS) Worker: The person assigned to a report of child maltreatment at the time of the report disposition.

Child Protective Services (CPS) Workforce: The CPS supervisors and workers assigned to handle a child maltreatment report. May include other administrative staff, as defined by the state agency.

Child Record: A case-level record in the child file containing the data associated with one child in one report.

Child Victim: A child for whom an incident of abuse or neglect has been substantiated or indicated by an investigation or assessment. A state may include some children with alternative dispositions as victims.

Children's Bureau: Federal agency within the Administration on Children, Youth and Families, Administration for Children and Families, U.S. Department of Health & Human Services.

Child's Living Arrangement: The home environment in which the child was residing at the time of the report (for example, family or substitute care).

Closed with No Finding: Disposition that does not conclude with a specific finding because the investigation could not be completed for such reasons as: The family moved out of the jurisdiction; the family could not be located; or necessary diagnostic or other reports were not received within required time limits.

CNS Depressants: A class of drugs that slow CNS (Central Nervous System) functions, some of which are used to treat anxiety and sleeping disorders; includes barbiturates and benzodiazepines.

Coca: The plant, *Erythroxylon*, from which cocaine is derived. Also refers to the leaves of this plant.

Cocaethylene: Potent stimulant created when cocaine and alcohol are used together.

Cocaine: A highly addictive stimulant drug derived from the coca plant that produces profound feelings of pleasure.

Community-Based Family Resource and Support Grant: Grant provided under Section 210 of the Child Abuse Prevention and Treatment Act (CAPTA) that assists states in preventing child abuse and neglect and promoting positive development of parents and children by developing, operating, expanding and enhancing a network of community-based, prevention-focused, family resource and support programs that coordinate resources among a broad range of human service organizations.

Court Action: Legal action initiated by a representative of the Child Protective Services agency on behalf of the child. This includes authorization to place the child in foster care and filing for temporary custody, dependency, or termination of parental rights. It does not include criminal proceedings against a perpetrator.

Court-Appointed Representative: A person appointed by the court to represent a child in a neglect or abuse proceeding. May be an attorney or a Court-Appointed Special Advocate (or both) and is often referred to as a guardian *ad litem*. The representative makes recommendations to the court concerning the best interests of the child.

Court-Appointed Special Advocate (CASA): Adult volunteers trained to advocate for abused and neglected children who are involved in the juvenile court.

Crack: Slang term for a smokable form of cocaine.

Depressants: Drugs that relieve anxiety and produce sleep. Depressants include barbiturates, benzodiazepines, and alcohol.

Designer Drug: An analog of a restricted drug that has psychoactive properties.

Detoxification: A process of allowing the body to rid itself of a drug while managing the symptoms of withdrawal; often the first step in a drug treatment program.

Dextromethorphan: A cough-suppressing ingredient in a variety of over-the-counter cold and cough medications abused for its intoxicating effects. Also called *DXM* and *Robo*.

Differential Response: An area of Child Protective Services reform that offers greater flexibility in responding to allegations of abuse and neglect. Also referred to as "dual track" or "multi-track" response, it permits CPS agencies to respond differentially to children's needs for safety, the degree of risk present, and the family's needs for services and support. *(See Dual Track.)*

Disposition: *See Investigation Disposition.*

Drug: A chemical compound or substance that can alter the structure and function of the body. Psychoactive drugs affect the function of the brain and some of these may be illegal to use and possess.

Drug Abuse: The use of illegal drugs or the inappropriate use of legal drugs. The repeated use of drugs to produce pleasure, to alleviate stress, or to alter or avoid reality (or all three).

Dual Track: Term reflecting Child Protective Services response systems that typically combine a non-adversarial, service-based assessment track for cases where children are not at immediate risk with a traditional CPS investigative track for cases where children are unsafe or at greater risk for maltreatment. *(See Differential Response.)*

DXM: Common street name for dextromethorphan.

Ecstasy (MDMA): A chemically modified amphetamine that has hallucinogenic as well as stimulant properties.

Educational Personnel: Employees of a public or private educational institution or program; includes teachers, teacher assistants, administrators, and others directly associated with the delivery of educational services.

Family Assessment: The stage of the child protection process when the Child Protective Services caseworker, community treatment provider, and the family reach a mutual understanding regarding the behaviors and conditions that must

  The Parent's Guide to Helping Teenagers in Crisis

change to reduce or eliminate the risk of maltreatment, the most critical treatment needs that must be addressed, and the strengths on which to build.

Family Group Conferencing Model: A family meeting model used by Child Protective Services agencies to optimize family strengths in the planning process. This model brings together the family, extended family, and others important in the family's life (for example, friends, clergy, or neighbors) to make decisions regarding how best to ensure safety of the family members.

Family Preservation Services: Activities designed to help families alleviate crises that might lead to out-of-home placement of children, maintain the safety of children in their own homes, support families preparing to reunify or adopt, and assist families in obtaining services and other supports necessary to address their multiple needs in a culturally sensitive manner.

Family Support Services: Community-based preventive activities designed to alleviate stress and promote parental competencies and behaviors that will increase the ability of families to nurture their children successfully, enable families to use other resources and opportunities available in the community, and create supportive networks to enhance childrearing abilities of parents.

Family Unity Model: A family meeting model used by Child Protective Services agencies to optimize family strengths in the planning process. This model is similar to the Family Group Conferencing model.

Fatality: Death of a child as a result of abuse or neglect; because either an injury resulting from the abuse or neglect was the cause of death, or abuse or neglect were contributing factors to the cause of death.

Foster Care: Twenty-four-hour substitute care for children placed away from their parents or guardians and for whom the state agency has placement and care responsibility. This includes family foster homes, foster homes of relatives, group homes, emergency shelters, residential facilities, child-care institutions, and pre-adoptive homes, regardless of whether the facility is licensed and whether payments are made by the state or local agency for the care of the child, or whether there is federal matching of any payments made. Foster care may be provided by those who are related or those who are unrelated to the child. All children in care for more than 24 hours are counted.

Foster Parent: An individual licensed to provide a home for orphaned, abused, neglected, delinquent, or disabled children, usually with the approval of the government or a social service agency. May be a relative or non-relative acquainted with the child, the parent, or caregiver, including landlords, clergy, or youth group workers (for example, Scout leaders or Little League coaches).

Full Disclosure: Child Protective Services information given to the family regarding the steps in the intervention process, the requirements of CPS, the expectations of the family, the consequences if the family does not fulfill the expectations, and the rights of the parents to ensure that the family completely understands the process.

Girl: A female child younger than 18 years old.

Group Home or Residential Care: A non-familial, 24-hour care facility that may be supervised by the state agency or governed privately.

Guardian *ad litem*: A lawyer or layperson representing a child in juvenile or family court. Usually this person considers the "best interest" of the child and may perform a variety of roles, including those of independent investigator, advocate, advisor, and guardian for the child. A layperson who serves in this role is sometimes known as a Court-Appointed Special Advocate (CASA). *(See Court-Appointed Representative.)*

Hallucinogens: A diverse group of drugs that alter perceptions, thoughts, and feelings. Hallucinogenic drugs include LSD, mescaline, MDMA (ecstasy), PCP, and psilocybin (magic mushrooms).

Heroin: The potent, widely abused opiate that produces addiction. It consists of two morphine molecules linked together chemically.

Home Visitation Programs: Prevention programs that offer a variety of family-focused services to pregnant mothers and families with new babies. Activities frequently encompass structured visits to the family's home and may address positive parenting practices, nonviolent discipline techniques, child development, maternal and child health, available services, and advocacy.

Immunity: Established in all child abuse laws to protect reporters from civil law suits and criminal prosecution resulting from filing a report of child abuse and neglect.

Indicated or Reason to Suspect: An investigation disposition that concludes that maltreatment cannot be substantiated under state law or policy, but there is reason to suspect the child may have been maltreated or was at risk of maltreatment. This is applicable only to states that distinguish between substantiated and indicated dispositions.

Inhalant: Any drug administered by breathing in its vapors. Inhalants commonly are organic solvents, such as glue and paint thinner, or anesthetic gases, such as ether and nitrous oxide.

Initial Assessment or Investigation: The stage of the Child Protective Services (CPS) case process where the CPS caseworker determines the validity of the child maltreatment report; assesses the risk of maltreatment; determines if the child is safe; develops a safety plan, if needed, to assure the child's protection; and determines services needed. If face-to-face contact with the alleged victim isn't possible, then the initial investigation is when CPS first contacts any party who can provide information essential to the investigation or assessment.

Intake: The activities associated with the receipt of a referral, the assessment or screening, the decision to accept, and the enrollment of individuals or families into services.

Intentionally False: The unsubstantiated investigation disposition that indicates a conclusion that the person who made the allegation of maltreatment knew the allegation was not true.

Interview Protocol: A structured format to ensure that all family members are seen in a planned strategy, that community providers collaborate, and that information gathering is thorough.

Investigation: The gathering and assessment of objective information to determine if a child has been or is at risk of being maltreated. Generally includes face-to-face contact with the victim and results in a disposition as to whether or not the alleged report is substantiated.

Investigation Disposition: A determination made by a social service agency that evidence is or is not sufficient under state law to conclude that maltreatment occurred.

Investigation Disposition Date: The point in time at the end of the investigation or assessment when a Child Protective Services worker declares a disposition to the child maltreatment report.

Investigation Start Date: The date when Child Protective Services initially contacted or attempted to have face-to-face contact with the alleged victim. If this face-to-face contact isn't possible, the date is when CPS initially contacts any party who can provide information essential to the investigation or assessment.

Juvenile and Family Courts: Established in most states to resolve conflict and to intervene otherwise in the lives of families in a manner that promotes the best interest of children. These courts specialize in areas such as child maltreatment, domestic violence, juvenile delinquency, divorce, child custody, and child support.

Kinship Care: Formal child placement by the juvenile court and child welfare agency in the home of a child's relative.

Legal Guardian: An adult with legal custody and guardianship of a minor.

Legal, Law Enforcement, or Criminal Justice Personnel: People employed by a local, state, tribal, or federal justice agency including law enforcement, courts, district attorney's office, probation or other community corrections agencies, and correctional facilities.

Liaison: The designation of a person within an organization who has responsibility for facilitating communication, collaboration, and coordination between agencies involved in the child protection system.

Living Arrangement: *See Child's Living Arrangement.*

LSD (Lysergic Acid Diethylamide): A hallucinogenic drug that acts on the serotonin receptor.

Maltreatment Type: A particular form of child maltreatment determined by investigation to be substantiated or indicated under state law. Types include physical abuse, neglect or deprivation of necessities, medical neglect, sexual abuse, psychological or emotional maltreatment, and other forms included in state law.

Mandated Reporter: Individuals required by state statutes to report suspected child abuse and neglect to the proper authorities (usually Child Protective Services or law enforcement agencies). Mandated reporters typically include professionals such as educators and other school personnel, health care and mental health professionals, social workers, childcare providers, and law enforcement officers. Some states identify all citizens as mandated reporters.

Marijuana: A drug, usually smoked but can be eaten, that is made from the leaves of the cannabis plant. The main psychoactive ingredient is THC.

MDMA (Ecstasy): Common chemical name for 3,4-methylenedioxymethamphetamine.

Medical Neglect: A type of maltreatment caused by failure of the caregiver to provide for the appropriate health care of the child although financially able to do so or offered financial or other means to do so.

Medical Personnel: People employed by a medical facility or practice, including physicians, physician assistants, nurses, emergency medical technicians, dentists, chiropractors, coroners, and dental assistants and technicians.

Medication: A drug used to treat an illness or disease according to established medical guidelines.

Mental Health Organization: An administratively distinct public or private agency or institution whose primary concern is the provision of direct mental health services to the mentally ill or emotionally disturbed.

- *Freestanding psychiatric outpatient clinics* provide only outpatient services on either a regular or emergency basis. The medical responsibility for services is generally assumed by a psychiatrist.

- *General hospitals providing separate psychiatric services* are non-federal general hospitals that provide psychiatric services in a separate psychiatric inpatient, outpatient, or partial hospitalization service with assigned staff and space.

- *Multiservice mental health organizations* directly provide two or more of the program elements defined under Mental Health Service Type and are not classifiable as a psychiatric hospital, general hospital, or a residential treatment center for emotionally disturbed children.

- *Partial care organizations* provide a program of ambulatory mental health services.

- *Private mental hospitals* are operated by a sole proprietor, partnership, limited partnership, corporation, or nonprofit organization primarily for the care of persons with mental disorders.

- *Psychiatric hospitals are hospitals* primarily concerned with providing inpatient care and treatment for the mentally ill.

- *Residential treatment centers for emotionally disturbed children* must meet all of the following criteria:

  (a) Not licensed as a psychiatric hospital, and its primary purpose is to provide individually planned mental health treatment services in conjunction with residential care.

  (b) Includes a clinical program that is directed by a psychiatrist, psychologist, social worker, or psychiatric nurse with a graduate degree.

  (c) Serves children and youth primarily under the age of 18.

  (d) The primary diagnosis for the majority of admissions is mental illness, classified as other than mental retardation, developmental disability, and substance-related disorders.

- *State and county mental hospitals* are under the auspices of a state or county government or operated jointly by a state and county government.

Mental Health Personnel: People employed by a mental health facility or practice, including psychologists, psychiatrists, and therapists.

Mental Health Service Type: Refers to the following kinds of mental health services—

- *Inpatient care* is the provision of 24-hour mental health care in a mental health hospital setting.

- *Outpatient care* is the provision of ambulatory mental health services for less than three hours at a single visit on an individual, group, or family basis, usually in a clinic or similar organization. Emergency care provided on a walk-in basis, as well as care provided by mobile teams who visit patients outside these organizations are included.

- *Partial care treatment* is a planned program of mental health treatment services generally provided in visits of three or more hours to groups of patients. Included are treatment programs that emphasize intensive short-term therapy and rehabilitation; programs that focus on recreation or occupational program activities, including sheltered workshops; and education and training programs, including special education classes, therapeutic nursery schools, and vocational training.

- *Residential treatment care* is the provision of overnight mental health care in conjunction with an intensive treatment program in a setting other than a hospital. Facilities may offer care to emotionally disturbed children or mentally ill adults.

Methadone: A long-acting synthetic medication that is effective in treating opioid (opiate) addiction.

Methamphetamine: A commonly abused, potent stimulant drug that is part of a larger family of amphetamines.

Multidisciplinary Team: Established between agencies and professionals within the child protection system to discuss cases of child abuse and neglect and to aid in decisions at various stages of the Child Protective Services case process. These terms may also be designated by different names, including *child protection teams, interdisciplinary teams,* or *case consultation teams.*

NCANDS: The National Child Abuse and Neglect Data System.

Neglect or Deprivation of Necessities: A type of maltreatment that refers to the failure by the caregiver to provide needed, age-appropriate care although financially able to do so or offered financial or other means to do so.

- *Physical neglect* can include not providing adequate food, clothing, appropriate medical care, supervision, or proper weather protection (heat or coats).

- *Educational neglect* includes failure to provide appropriate schooling or special educational needs, or allowing excessive truancies.

- *Psychological neglect* includes the lack of any emotional support and love, chronic inattention to the child, exposure to spouse abuse, or drug and alcohol abuse.

Neighbor: A person living in close geographical proximity to the child or family.

Noncaregiver: A person who is not responsible for the care and supervision of the child, including school personnel, friends, and neighbors.

Nonparent: Includes other relatives, foster parents, residential facility staff, child daycare provider, foster care provider, unmarried partner of parent, legal guardian, and "other."

Notifiable Disease: A notifiable disease is one that, when diagnosed, health providers are required, usually by law, to report to state or local public health officials. Notifiable diseases are those of public interest by reason of their contagiousness, severity, or frequency.

Opioids: Controlled drugs or narcotics most often prescribed for the management of pain; natural or synthetic chemicals based on opium's active component, morphine, that work by mimicking the actions of pain-relieving chemicals produced in the body.

Out-of-Court Contact: A meeting, which is not part of the actual judicial hearing, between the court-appointed representative and the child victim. Such contacts enable the court-appointed representative to obtain a firsthand understanding of the situation and needs of the child victim and to make recommendations to the court concerning the best interests of the child.

Out-of-Home Care: Child care, foster care, or residential care provided by persons, organizations, and institutions to children who are placed outside their families, usually under the jurisdiction of juvenile or family court.

***Parens Patriae* Doctrine:** Originating in feudal England, a doctrine that vests in the state a right of guardianship of minors. This concept has gradually evolved into the principle that the community, in addition to the parent, has a strong interest in the care and nurturing of children. Schools, juvenile courts, and social service agencies all derive their authority from the state's power to ensure the protection and rights of children as a unique class.

Parent: The birth mother or father, adoptive mother or father, or stepmother or father of the child victim.

PCP: Phencyclidine, a dissociative anesthetic abused for its mind-altering effects.

Perpetrator: The person who has been determined to have caused or knowingly allowed the maltreatment of a child.

Perpetrator Age: Age of an individual determined to have caused or knowingly allowed the maltreatment of a child. Age is calculated in years at the time of the report of child maltreatment.

Perpetrator Relationship: Primary role of the perpetrator to a child victim.

Physical Abuse: Type of maltreatment that refers to non-accidental physical acts that caused or could have caused physical injury to a child. This may include burning, hitting, punching, shaking, kicking, beating, or otherwise harming a child. It also may have been the result of over-discipline or physical punishment inappropriate to the child's age.

Physical Dependence: An adaptive physiological state that occurs with regular drug use and results in a withdrawal syndrome when drug use is stopped; usually occurs with tolerance.

Placebo: An inactive substance used in experiments to distinguish between actual drug effects and effects that are expected by the volunteers in the experiments.

Polydrug User: An individual who uses more than one drug.

Post-Investigation Services: Activities provided or arranged by the Child Protective Services agency, social services agency, or the child welfare agency for the child or family as a result of needs discovered during the course of an investigation. Includes such services as family preservation, family support, and foster care. Post-investigation services are delivered within the first 90 days after the disposition of the report.

Prescription Drug Abuse: The intentional misuse of a medication outside of the normally accepted standards of its use.

Prescription Drug Misuse: Taking a medication in a manner other than that prescribed or for a different condition than that for which the medication is prescribed.

Preventive Services: Activities aimed at preventing child abuse and neglect. Such activities may be directed at specific populations identified as being at increased risk of becoming abusive and may be designed to increase the strength and stability of families, to increase parents' confidence and competence in their parenting abilities, and to afford children a stable and supportive environment. They include child abuse and neglect preventive services provided through such federal funds as the Child Abuse and Neglect Basic State Grant, Community-based Family Resource and Support Grant, the Promoting Safe and Stable Families Program (title IV-B, subpart 2), Maternal and Child Health Block Grant, Social Services Block Grant (title XX), and state and local funds. Such activities do not include public awareness campaigns.

Primary Prevention: Activities geared to a sample of the general population to prevent child abuse and neglect from occurring. Also referred to as *universal prevention.*

Prior Child Victim: A child victim with previous substantiated, indicated, or alternative response reports of maltreatment.

Promoting Safe and Stable Families Program: Program that provides grants to the states under Section 430, title IV–B, subpart 2 of the Social Security Act, as amended, to develop and expand four types of services—community-based family support services; innovative child welfare services, including family preservation services; time-limited reunification services; and adoption promotion and support services.

Protective Factors: Strengths and resources that appear to mediate or serve as a "buffer" against risk factors, which contribute to vulnerability to maltreatment or against the negative effects of maltreatment experiences.

Protocol: An interagency agreement that delineates joint roles and responsibilities by establishing criteria and procedures for working together on cases of child abuse and neglect.

Psychedelic Drug: A drug that distorts perception, thought, and feeling. This term is typically used to refer to drugs with actions like those of LSD.

Psychoactive: Having a specific effect on the mind.

Psychoactive Drug: A drug that changes the way the brain works.

Psychological or Emotional Maltreatment: Type of maltreatment that refers to acts or omissions, other than physical abuse or sexual abuse, that caused, or could have caused, conduct, cognitive, affective, or other mental disorders. Includes emotional neglect, psychological abuse, and mental injury. Frequently occurs as a pattern of verbal abuse or excessive demands on a child's performance that convey to children that they are worthless, flawed, unloved, unwanted, endangered, or only of value to meeting another's needs. This can include parents or caretakers using extreme or bizarre forms of punishment or threatening or terrorizing a child. The term "psychological maltreatment" is also known as emotional abuse or neglect, verbal abuse, or mental abuse.

Psychotherapeutics: Drugs that have an effect on the function of the brain and that are often used to treat psychiatric disorders can include opioids, CNS depressants, and stimulants.

Race: The primary taxonomic category of which the individual identifies himself or herself as a member, or of which the parent identifies the child as a member (namely: American Indian or Alaska Native, Asian, Black or African-American, Hispanic or Latino, Native Hawaiian or Other Pacific Islander, White, or Unable to Determine).

Receipt of Report: The log-in of a referral to the agency alleging child maltreatment.

Referral: Notification to the Child Protective Services agency of suspected child maltreatment. This can include one or more children.

Relapse: In drug abuse, relapse is the resumption of drug use after trying to stop taking drugs. Relapse is a common occurrence in many chronic disorders, including addiction, that require behavioral adjustments to treat effectively.

Relative: A person connected to the child by blood, such as parents, siblings, or grandparents.

Report: A referral of child abuse or neglect that was accepted for an investigation or assessment by a Child Protective Services agency.

Report Date: The month, day, and year that the responsible agency was notified of the suspected child maltreatment.

Report Disposition: The conclusion reached by the responsible agency regarding the report of maltreatment pertaining to the child.

Report Source: The category or role of the person who notifies a Child Protective Services agency of alleged child maltreatment.

Residential Facility Staff: Employees of a public or private group residential facility, including emergency shelters, group homes, and institutions.

Response Time with Respect to the Initial Investigation: A determination made by Child Protective Services and law enforcement regarding the immediacy of the response needed to file a report of child abuse or neglect. Also the time between the log-in of a call alleging child maltreatment to the state agency and the face-to-face contact with the alleged victim where appropriate (or to be in contact with another person who can provide information when direct contact with the alleged victim would be inappropriate).

Response Time with Respect to the Provision of Services: The time from the log-in of a call to the agency alleging child maltreatment to the provision of post-investigation services, often requiring the opening of a case for ongoing services.

Review Hearings: Held by the juvenile and family court to review dispositions (usually every six months) and to determine the need to maintain placement in out-of-home care or court jurisdiction of a child.

Risk: The likelihood that a child will be maltreated in the future.

Risk Assessment: To assess and measure the likelihood that a child will be maltreated in the future, frequently through the use of checklists, matrices, scales, and other methods of measurement.

Risk Factors: Behaviors and conditions present in the child, parent, or family that will likely contribute to child maltreatment occurring in the future.

Robo: Common street name for dextromethorphan.

Safety: Absence of an imminent or immediate threat of moderate-to-serious harm to the child.

Safety Assessment: A part of the Child Protective Services case process in which available information is analyzed to identify whether a child is in immediate danger of moderate or serious harm.

Safety Plan: A casework document developed when it is determined that the child is in imminent or potential risk of serious harm. In the safety plan, the caseworker targets the factors causing or contributing to the risk of imminent serious harm to the child and identifies, along with the family, the interventions that will control the safety factors and assure the child's protection.

Screened-In Reports: Referrals of child maltreatment that met the state's standards for acceptance.

Screened-Out Referral: Allegations of child maltreatment that did not meet the state's standards for acceptance.

Screening: The process of making a decision about whether or not to accept a referral of child maltreatment.

Secondary Prevention: Activities targeted to prevent breakdowns and dysfunctions among families identified as at-risk for abuse and neglect.

Service Agreement: The casework document developed between the Child Protective Services caseworker and the family that outlines the tasks necessary to achieve goals and outcomes necessary for risk reduction.

Service Date: The date activities began as a result of needs discovered during the Child Protective Services response.

Service Provision: The stage of the Child Protective Services casework process when CPS and other service providers provide specific services geared toward the reduction of risk of maltreatment.

Services: Non-investigative public or private nonprofit activities provided or continued as a result of an investigation or assessment.

Sexual Abuse: A type of maltreatment that refers to the involvement of the child in sexual activity to provide sexual gratification or financial benefit to the adolescent or adult perpetrator, including contacts for sexual purposes by fondling a child's genitals, making the child fondle the adult's genitals, intercourse, molestation, statutory rape, prostitution, pornography, exposure, exhibitionism, incest, sodomy, exposure to pornography, or other sexually exploitative activities. To be considered child abuse, these acts have to be committed by a person responsible for the care of a child (for example a baby-sitter, a parent, or a daycare provider) or related to the child. If a stranger commits these acts, it would be considered sexual assault and handled solely by the police and criminal courts.

Social Services Block Grant: Funds provided by title XX of the Social Security Act that are used for services to the states, which may include child care, child protection, child and foster care services, and daycare.

Social Services Personnel: Employees of a public or private social service or social welfare agency, or other social worker or counselor who provides similar services.

State Agency: The agency in a state that is responsible for child protection and child welfare.

Stepparent: The husband or wife, by a subsequent marriage, of the child's mother or father.

Stimulants: A class of drugs that elevates mood, increases feelings of well-being, and increases energy and alertness. These drugs produce euphoria and are powerfully rewarding. Stimulants include cocaine, methamphetamine, and methylphenidate (Ritalin).

Substantiated: A type of investigation disposition that concludes the allegation of maltreatment or risk of maltreatment was supported or founded by state law or state policy. A Child Protective Services determination means that credible evidence exists that child abuse or neglect has occurred. This is the highest level of finding by a state agency.

Systems of Care: A system of care is a process of partnering an array of service agencies and families, working together to provide individualized care and supports designed to help children and families achieve safety, stability, and permanency in their home and community.

Tertiary Prevention: Treatment efforts geared toward addressing situations where child maltreatment has already occurred and with the goals of preventing child maltreatment from occurring in the future and of avoiding the harmful effects of child maltreatment.

THC: Delta-9-tetrahydrocannabinol; the main active ingredient in marijuana that acts on the brain to produce its effects.

Tolerance: A condition in which higher doses of a drug are required to produce the same effect as during initial use; often leads to physical dependence.

Toxic: Temporary or permanent drug effects that are detrimental to the functioning of an organ or group of organs.

Tranquilizers: Drugs prescribed to promote sleep or reduce anxiety; this National Household Survey on Drug Abuse classification includes benzodiazepines, barbiturates, and other types of CNS depressants.

Treatment: The stage of the child protection case process when specific services are provided by Child Protective Services and other providers to reduce the risk of maltreatment, to support families in meeting case goals, and to address the effects of maltreatment.

Universal Prevention: Activities and services directed at the general public with the goal of stopping the occurrence of maltreatment before it starts. Also referred to as *primary prevention.*

Unmarried Partner of Parent: Someone who has a relationship with the parent and lives in the household with the parent and maltreated child.

Unsubstantiated (Not Substantiated): An investigation disposition that determines there is not sufficient evidence under state law or policy to conclude that the child has been maltreated or is at risk of maltreatment. A Child Protective Services determination means that credible evidence does not exist that child abuse or neglect has occurred.

Victim: A child having a maltreatment disposition of *substantiated, indicated,* or *alternative response victim.*

Withdrawal: Symptoms that occur after chronic use of a drug is reduced or stopped.

This information was compiled from the following sources—

Administration for Children and Families, U.S. Department of Health and Human Services, "Appendix B: Glossary—Child Maltreatment 2002", *Children's Bureau.*

Center for Disease Control and Prevention, National Center for Health Statistics, *Health United States,* 2004, "NCHS Definitions."

National Institute on Drug Abuse, *www.drugabuse.gov/NIDAHome.html*

U.S. Department of Health and Human Services, Administration for Children & Families, *Child Welfare Information Gateway* (formerly the National Clearinghouse on Child Abuse and Neglect Information and the National Adoption Information Clearinghouse). Available online at *http://www.childwelfare.gov/*

7.0

ENDNOTES

1.1 | Is This a Crisis or Isn't It?

1. Gary Collins, *How to Be a People Helper* (Santa Ana, Calif.: Vision House, 1976), 71.

2. Luke 13:4

3. Matthew 5:45

1.2 | Dangerous Opportunity

1. Madeleine L'Engle, excerpted in *Glimpses of Grace: Daily Thoughts and Reflections* (HarperSanFrancisco, 1998), 292.

2. 2 Corinthians 1:3-4

2.1 | *Triage*

1. Henri J. M. Nouwen, *Reaching Out* (New York: Doubleday, 1975), 94.

2. Luke 6:36

3. Psalm 34:18

4. Jim Hancock, *Raising Adults* (Leucadia, Calif.: Jim Hancock, 2007), 142-143. This eBook can be downloaded from the YS Underground Web site at: https://shop.youthspecialties.com/ysunderground/product.php?productid=1229&cat=0&page=1

2.3 | Connecting

1. Robert L. Veninga, *A Gift of Hope, How We Survive Our Tragedies* (New York: Ballantine Books, 1996), 60.

2. Michael Craig Miller, "How Important Is the Therapeutic Alliance?" *Questions & Answers*, Harvard Mental Health Letter. September 2004.

3. It's worth noting that Miller's emphasis here lives in tension with Karl Menninger's contention that diagnosis is the most important factor in successful treatment. Our hunch is that the two work in parallel: It's tough to get a good di-

agnosis without the beginnings of a strong working alliance; the right diagnosis increases the strength of the working alliance.

4. Proverbs 17:22

5. Ann Kaiser Stearns, *Living Through Personal Crisis* (Chicago: Thomas More Press, 1983), 93.

6. Jim Hancock, *Raising Adults* (Leucadia, Calif.: Jim Hancock, 2007). This eBook can be downloaded from the YS Underground Web site at: https://shop.youth-specialties.com/ysunderground/product.php?productid=1229&cat=0&page=1

7. Veninga, 60.

2.4 | Deep Listening

1. M. Scott Peck, M.D., *The Road Less Traveled* (New York: Simon and Schuster, 1978), 121.

2. Proverbs 20:5

3. Peck, *The Road Less Traveled*, 121.

4. Barbara Varenhorst, *Real Friends: Becoming the Friend You'd Like to Have* (San Francisco: Harper and Row, 1983), 107.

5. Paul W. Swets, *The Art of Talking with Your Teenager* (Holbrook, Mass.: Adams Media Corporation, 1995), 86.

3.2 | Developing an Action Plan

1. Lee Ann Hoff, *People in Crisis: Understanding and Helping* (Menlo Park, Calif.: Addison-Wesley, 1978), 56-60.

2. Ann Landers, *The Denver Post*, April 8, 1985.

3. John 5:6

3.3 | *Interventions*

1. Alan I. Leshner, National Institute on Drug Abuse, *The Science of Drug Abuse and Addiction*, "The Essence of Drug Addiction," www.drugabuse.gov/Published_Articles/Essence.html (Web page last updated June 14, 2005; accessed June 3, 2007).

2. From a conversation with Jim Hancock.

4.3 | Bullying

1. *Bullying Among Young Adolescents: The Strong, the Weak, and the Troubled*, DOI: 10.1542/peds.112.6.1231; Pediatrics 2003:112;1231-1237, Jaana Juvonen, Sandra Graham and Mark A. Schuster, http://pediatrics.aappublications.org/cgi/content/full/112/6/1231 (accessed June 3, 2007).

4.6 | Death

1. Elisabeth Kübler-Ross, *On Death and Dying* (New York: Touchstone, 1969).

4.7 | Divorce

1. Mary Elizabeth Giffin, M.D. and Carol Felsenthal, *A Cry for Help* (Garden City, N.Y.: Doubleday, 1983), 153.

2. David Elkind, *All Grown Up and No Place to Go: Teenagers in Crisis* (New York: Perseus Books Group; rev. ed., 1997), 130.

3. Warner Troyer, *Divorced Kids* (New York: Harcourt, Brace, Jovanovich, 1979), 166.

4.8 | Dropping Out

1. U.S. Department of Education, "Departments of Justice and Education Host National Truancy Prevention Conference," press release, December 6, 2004,

www.ed.gov/news/pressreleases/2004/12/12062004.html (accessed June 3, 2007).

2. Bob Herbert, Education, Education, Education, *New York Times*, March 5, 2007, Op Ed.

4.9 | Eating Disorders

1. Forum on Child and Family Statistics, "America's Children in Brief: Key National Indicators of Well-Being, 2006," http://www.childstats.gov/americaschildren/hea.asp#overweight (accessed June 3, 2007).

2. Pam W. Vredevelt and Joyce R. Whitman, *Walking a Thin Line: Anorexia and Bulimia, The Battle Can Be Won* (Portland, Ore.: Multnomah, 1985), 29-31.

4.10 | Hazing

1. Nadine C. Hoover and Norman J. Pollard, *Initiation Rites in American High Schools: A National Survey* (Alfred, N.Y.: Alfred University, August 2000). Also available online at http://www.alfred.edu/hs_hazing/ (accessed June 3, 2007).

4.11 | Incest

1. Diana E. H. Russell, Introduction to *The Secret Trauma: Incest in the Lives of Girls and Women* (New York: BasicBooks/Perseus Press, 1999), xvii.

2. M. Glasser, I. Kolvin, D. Campbell, A. Glasser, I. Leitch and S. Farrelly, "Cycle of Child Sexual Abuse: Links between Being a Victim and Becoming a Perpetrator," *The British Journal of Psychiatry* 179 (2001): 482-494.

3. New York City Alliance Against Sexual Assault, Alliance: Factsheets: Incest. Copyright 1997. Available online at www.nycagainstrape.org/printable/printable_survivors_factsheet_37.html (accessed June 3, 2007).

4. Ruth S. Kempe and C. Henry Kempe, *The Common Secret: Sexual Abuse of Children and Adolescents* (New York: W.H. Freeman, 1984), 86.

5. Donna Pence and Charles Wilson, *The Role of Law Enforcement in the Response to Child Abuse and Neglect* (U.S. Department of Health & Human Services, National Center on Child Abuse and Neglect, 1992), 18.

4.12 | Post-Traumatic Stress Disorder (PTSD)

1. National Institute of Mental Health Fact Sheet, Publication No. OM-99 4157 (2002 Revised); and Disaster Mental Health Response Handbook, State Health Publication No: (CMH) 00145, Centre for Mental Health and the New South Wales Institute of Psychiatry, North Sydney, NSW, Australia, 2000.

2. National Institute of Mental Health, "Facts About Post-Traumatic Stress Disorder," Publication No. OM-99 4157 (Revised) 2002, 2.

4.15 | Sexual Abuse

1. Administration for Children and Families, U.S. Department of Health and Human Services, "Appendix B: Glossary—Child Maltreatment 2002", *Children's Bureau*. http://www.acf.hhs.gov/programs/cb/systems/ncands/ncands98/glossary/glossary.htm (Web page last updated on May 11, 2006 and accessed June 4, 2007).

2. U.S. Department of Health and Human Services, Child Welfare Information Gateway (formerly the National Clearinghouse on Child Abuse and Neglect Information), Glossary – S. http://www.childwelfare.gov/pubs/usermanuals/domesticviolence/domesticviolenceh.cfm#s (Web page last updated on March 26, 2007 and accessed June 3, 2007).

3. Ibid.

4. Legal Information Institute, "§ 2256 Definitions for chapter," *U.S. Code Collection*. Release date: August 6, 2004. http://assembler.law.cornell.edu/uscode/html/uscode18/usc_sec_18_00002256----000-.html (accessed June 3, 2007).

5. W. Prendergast in *The Merry-Go-Round of Sexual Abuse: Identifying and Treating Suvivors* (New York: Haworth Press, 1993), as cited in M. Glasser, et al., "Cycle of Child Sexual Abuse," *The British Journal of Psychiatry* 179 (2001): 491.

6. Howard N. Snyder, Ph.D., "Sexual Assault of Young Children as Reported to Law Enforcement: Victim, Incident and Offender Characteristics," *Bureau of Justice Statistics* (U.S. Department of Justice and Office of Justice Programs, NCJ 182990, July 2000), 4. Also available online at: http://www.ojp.usdoj.gov/bjs/pub/pdf/saycrle.pdf (accessed June 3, 2007).

7. Ibid.

8. U.S. Department of Justice, Bureau of Justice Statistics, "Summary Findings," *Crime Characteristics*. Available online at: www.ojp.usdoj.gov/bjs/cvict_c. htm#relate (Web page last updated April 18, 2007 and accessed June 3, 2007).

4.16 | Sexual Identity Confusion

1. Barbara L. Frankowski, M.D., M.P.H. and American Academy of Pediatrics Committee on Adolescence, "Sexual Orientation and Adolescents," *Pediatrics* 113, No. 6 (June 2004), 1827-1832. Available online at www.pediatrics.org/cgi/content/full/113/6/1827 (accessed June 3, 2007).

4.17 | Sexually Transmitted Diseases (STDs)

1. Alan Guttmacher Institute, *Facts in Brief*, "Teen Sex and Pregnancy," Revised September 1999.

4.18 | Substance Abuse + Addiction

1. Centers for Disease Control and Prevention, Surveillance Summaries June 9, 2006 / Vol. 55 / No. SS-5. Every two years the survey is conducted during the spring semester in a representative sample of ninth through twelfth graders in public and private schools. The most current reports are available athttp://www. cdc.gov/mmwr/PDF/SS/SS5505.pdf (accessed July 5, 2007).

2. T. Santibanez, L. Barker, J. Santoli, C. Bridges, G. Euler, and M. McCauley, "Alcohol-Attributable Deaths and Years of Potential Life Lost—United States, 2001," *Morbidity and Mortality Weekly Report* 53, no. 37 (September 24, 2004): 866. Available online at http://www.findarticles.com/p/articles/mi_m0906/is_37_53/ai_n6256683 (accessed June 3, 2007).

3. *Tenth Special Report to Congress on Alcohol and Health from the Secretary of Human Services* (June 2000), DHHS Publication No. 00-1583.

4. A. Hyland, C. Vena, J. Bauer, Q. Li, G.A. Giovino, J. Yang, K.M. Cummings, P. Mowery, J. Fellows, T. Pechacek and L. Pederson, "Cigarette Smoking-Attributable Morbidity—United States, 2000" *Morbidity and Mortality Weekly Report* 52, no. 35 (September 5, 2003): 842. Available online at http://www.findarticles. com/p/articles/mi_m0906/is_35_52/ai_109443279 (accessed June 3, 2007).

5. James Baldwin, *James Baldwin: Collected Essays : Notes of a Native Son / Nobody Knows My Name / The Fire Next Time / No Name in the Street / The Devil Finds Work / Other Essays,* Library of America, 1998, 173.

6. David Elkind, *All Grown Up and No Place to Go: Teenagers in Crisis* (New York: Perseus Books Group; rev. ed., 1997), 21.

7. Dr. Gary G. Forrest, *How to Cope with a Teenage Drinker* (New York: Scribner, 1983), 1.

8. See Mary E. Larimer and Jessica M. Cronce, *Journal of Studies on Alcohol,* Supplement no. 14 (2002): 152.

9. Alan I. Leshner, National Institute on Drug Abuse, *The Science of Drug Abuse and Addiction,* "The Essence of Drug Addiction," www.drugabuse.gov/Published_Articles/Essence.html (Web page last updated June 14, 2005; accessed June 3, 2007).

4.19 | Suicide

1. Salman Rushdie, *The Ground Beneath Her Feet,* Picador, 2000, 206.

2. National Institute of Mental Health, "In Harm's Way: Suicide in America," NIH Publication No. 03-4594, Printed January 2001; Revised April 2003. Also, American Association of Suicidology, "United States Suicide Statistics," summarized and prepared by Dr. John L. McIntosh. Available online at www.suicidology.org/displaycommon.cfm?an=1&subarticlenbr=21 (accessed on June 3, 2007).

3. 2 Timothy 2:13

4.20 | Terror

1. Job 5:7

2. Ernest Hemingway, *A Farewell to Arms* (New York: Scribner's and Sons, 1957), 249.

4.21 | Trouble with the Law

1. Dr. Scott Larson, *At Risk: Bringing Hope to Hurting Teenagers* (Loveland, Colo.: Group, 1999), 49.

4.22 | Violence

1. Howard N. Snyder and Melissa Sickmund. *Juvenile Offenders and Victims: 2006 National Report*, Washington DC: U.S. Department of Justice, Office of Justice Programs, Office of Juvenile Justice and Delinquency Prevention, http://ojjdp.ncjrs.org/ojstatbb/nr2006/index.html (accessed June 4, 2007).

2. B. Vossekuil, R. Fein, M. Reddy, R. Borum, and W. Modzeleski, *The Final Report and Findings of the Safe School Initiative: Implications for the Prevention of School Attacks in the United States.* U.S. Department of Education, Office of Elementary and Secondary Education, Safe and Drug-Free Schools Program and U.S. Secret Service, National Threat Assessment Center, Washington DC, 2002, http://www.secretservice.gov/ntac/ssi_final_report.pdf (accessed June 4, 2007).

3. Donna L. Hoyert, Melonie P. Heron, Sherry L. Murphy, and Hsiang-Ching Kung, "Deaths: Final Data for 2003," National Vital Statistics Reports 54, no. 13 (April 19, 2006), http://www.cdc.gov/nchs/products/pubs/pubd/hestats/finaldeaths03/finaldeaths03.htm (Web page last reviewed on January 11, 2007, accessed June 4, 2007).

4. J. Doan, S. Roggenbaum, & K. Lazear. (2003). *Youth suicide prevention school-based guide(c/p/r/s)—True/False 1: Information dissemination in schools—The Facts about Adolescent Suicide.* Tampa, FL: Department of Child and Family Studies, Division of State and Local Support, Louis de la Parte Florida Mental Health Institute, University of South Florida. (FMHI Series Publication #219-1t), http://theguide.fmhi.usf.edu/pdf/True-false.pdf (accessed June 4, 2007).

5. U.S. Department of Justice, Office of Justice Programs, Bureau of Justice Statistics. *Homicide Trends in the U.S.: Weapons Used,* http://www.ojp.usdoj.gov/bjs/homicide/weapons.htm (Web page last updated June 29, 2006, accessed June 3, 2007).

6. C. S. Lewis, *Miracles* (New York: Macmillan, 1947), 111.

7. B. Vossekuil, et al., *The Final Report and Findings of the Safe School Initiative*, 22.

5.0 | Prevention Inside | Out

1. The Arthur C. Clarke Foundation at www.clarkefoundation.org/projects (accessed June 3, 2007).

5.1 | Inside Prevention: Building Resilience

1. Youth Peer Education Toolkit, *Training of Trainers Manual*, United Nations Population Fund, and Youth Peer Education Network (Y-PEER), 2005, 178.

5.2 | Outside Prevention: Building Preventive Partnerships

1. See, for example, Centers for Disease Control and Prevention, "Guidelines for Investigating Clusters of Health Events," Recommendations and Reports, *Morbidity and Mortality Weekly Report* 39(RR-11); 1-16. July 27, 1990. www.cdc.gov/mmwr/preview/mmwrhtml/00001797.htm (accessed June 3, 2007).

2. We're not endorsing this organization for its theology—the last time we looked at their Web site (www.capabilitiesinc.com/) they didn't have a corporate theology. We say this because sometimes parents say they want something explicitly *biblical*, to which we say, make it as explicitly biblical as you want. What *Developing Capable People* offers can easily be retrofitted with your theology unless you think the Bible gives you permission to treat children as slaves in which case it's hard to believe you got so far in *this* book. Seriously: Don't hurt the children. Depending on where you go, the DCP training of trainers can be expensive; but beyond that the costs are minimal and the benefits maximal.

5.3 | A Final Word

1. Paul's letter to the Galatians (chapter two, verses 15 - 21), if you're inclined to read other people's mail.

2. C.S. Lewis, *Letters of C.S. Lewis* (New York, Harcourt Brace Javanovich, 1966), 285.

3. Ernest Hemingway, *A Farewell to Arms* (New York. Scribner's and Sons, 1957), 249.

We may nevr fully understand teenagers, but we can learn more about them with *Youth Culture 101*. Cultural analyst and adolescent expert, Walt Mueller, shares research and trends to help you better understand yours students and minister to them more effectively in their ever changing world. It's an invaluable resource for youth ministry teams and parents of teenagers.

Youth Culture 101
Walt Mueller
Author Name
RETAIL $19.99
ISBN 0-310-27313-7

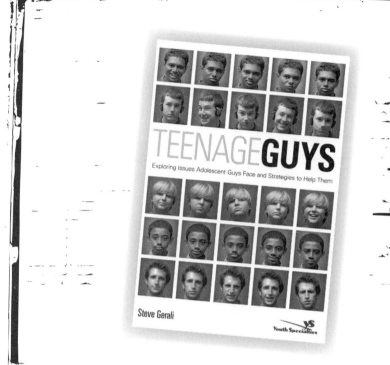

In *Teenager Guys*, author Steve Gerali breaks down the stages of development that adolescent guys go through, providing stories from his own experiences in ministry and counseling, as well as practical research findings to equip youth workers (both male and female) to more effectively minister to teenage guys. Each chapter includes advice from counselors and veteran youth workers, as well as discussion questions.

Teenage Guys
Exploring Issues Adolescent Guys Face and Strategies to Help Them
Steve Gerali
RETAIL $17.99
ISBN 0-310-26985-7

visit www.youthspecialties.com/store
or your local Christian bookstore

In *Teenager Girls*, you'll find advice from counselors and veteran youth workers, along with helpful suggestions on how to minister to teenage girls. In addition to the traditional issues people commonly associate with girls (eating disorders, self-image issues, depression, etc.), author Ginny Olson will guide you through some of the new issues on the rise in girls' lives.

Teenage Girls
Exploring Issues Adolescent Girls Face and Strategies to Help Them
Ginny Olson
RETAIL $17.99
ISBN 0-310-26632-7

youth
specialties

If you've ever wondered if God is really there and listening, if you're good enough, or what's so great about heaven, you're not alone. We all hav hard and personal questions, but the answers are often harder to come by. In this book, you'll discover how to navigate your big questions, and what the answers mean for your life and faith.

Living with Questions
Dale Fincher
RETAIL $9.99
ISBN 0-310-27664-0

**youth
specialties**

Listen to what Jesus has to say to you. In this 60-day devo
you'll receive daily letters from Jesus and spend some time
journaling your thoughts back to Him as you take part in the
conversation.

Conversations with Jesus
Getting in on God's Story
Youth for Christ
RETAIL $10.99
ISBN 0-310-27346-3

Visit www.invertbooks.com or your local bookstore.

Most teenagers think being a Christian means doing the right thing, but figuring out what the "right thing" is can be a challenge. It's difficult for students to tell the difference between God's plan for them and what other Christians say is God's plan for them. Author Mark Matlock will guide your students through God's Word to help them figure out what God really wants from them.

What Does God Want from Me?
Understanding God's Desire for Your Life
Mark Matlock
RETAIL $9.99
ISBN 0-310-25815-4

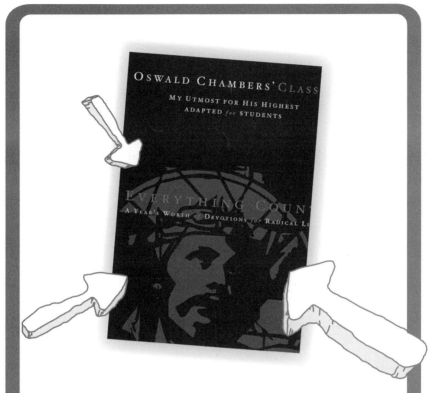

The classic Osward Chambers' My Utmost for His Highest adapted for students, this daily devotional dumps the pleasantries of religion and leads your students to real faith. Each day includes a Scripture reference, and excerpt from the classic text, and a phrase students can easily memorize to remind them about the reality of being a child of God.

Everything Counts
A Year's Worth of Devotions on Radical Living
Steven Case
RETAIL $14.99
ISBN 0-310-25408-6

Love This! contains real-life stories of people like you who've found ways to love their neighbors. It will challenge you to make a difference in your world by loving people who are often ignored or unloved—the homeless, the addicted, the elderly, those of different races, even your enemies—and show you tangible ways you can demonstrate that love.

Love This!
Learning to Make It a Way of Life, Not Just a Word
Andy Braner
RETAIL $12.99
ISBN 0-310-27380-3

Many people think teenagers aren't capable of much. But Zach Hunter is proving those people wrong. He's only fifteen, but he's working to end slavery in the world—and he's making changes that affect millions of people. Find out how Zach is making a difference and how you can make changes in the things that you see wrong with our world.

Be the Change
Your Guide to Freeing Slaves and Changing the World
Zach Hunter
RETAIL $9.99
ISBN 0-310-27756-6

It's not that you don't want to read the Bible; maybe you just don't know there's more than one way to read it.

Enjoy the Silence's 30 guided exercises plug you into the ancient discipline of lectio divina. Each lesson provides a selection of Scripture, prompts for meditation, a chance to listen to God, and a way to respond to what you've read.

Enjoy the Silence
A 30 Day Experiment in Listening to God
Maggie and Duffy Robbins
RETAIL $9.99
ISBN 0-310-25991-6

Visit www.invertbooks.com or your local bookstore.